Greenhill Books

THE WORLD'S ELITE FORCES

SMALL ARMS AND ACCESSORIES

GREENHILL MILITARY MANUALS

THE WORLD'S ELITE FORCES SMALL ARMS AND ACCESSORIES

GREENHILL MILITARY MANUALS

John Walter

Greenhill Books, London
Stackpole Books, Pennsylvania

For Alison and Adam, with love

Greenhill Books

This edition of *The World's Elite Forces: Small Arms and Accessories* first published 2002 by Greenhill Books,
Lionel Leventhal Limited, Park House, 1 Russell Gardens, London NW11 9NN
www.greenhillbooks.com
and
Stackpole Books, 5067 Ritter Road, Mechanicsburg, PA 17055, USA

British Library Cataloguing in Publication Data
Walter, John, 1951–
The world's elite forces: small arms and accessories. – (Greenhill military manuals)
1. Firearms 2. Special forces (Military science) – Equipment and supplies
I. Title
355.8'24

ISBN 1-85367-496-6

Library of Congress Cataloging-in-Publication Data available

Designed by John Anastasio, Creative Line, London
Printed and bound in Singapore by Kyodo Printing Company

Front cover illustration: The modern soldier must master sophisticated equipment such as night vision sights – even when wearing a gas mask!

INTRODUCTION

The modern counter-terrorist operative often comes dressed like a mediaeval warrior, complete with helmet and body armour. This man carries a Heckler & Koch MP5 with a light projector.

There is no such thing as the ideal weapon. Nation after nation has spent tens of years and colossal sums of money in pursuit of this particular grail; yet all attempts to provide the ultimate standardisation have been flawed. The US Army, in particular, has experimented with increasingly bizarre infantry weapons, with features that have included high-velocity flechette ammunition, integral grenade launchers and a variety of sights. Experimenters – and those who follow progress for professional reasons – have been confronted with a variety of abbreviations and acronyms (SPIW, OCIW, ACR, CAW) that cloak individual development goals.

These trials beg a question: why? It is well known that the global arms industry is extremely competitive and that there are great gains for the victors. And while it is undoubtedly true that the greatest spoils are the prerogative of the aircraft manufacturers, warship-builders and electronics conglomerates, success can percolate down to the humblest maker of guns, sights and ammunition.

Each generation has seen great successes and equally spectacular failures. Designs such as the Maxim machine-gun or the Bren Gun have been instantaneous successes, but most others, if they have seen success at all, have done so only after protracted development and an appreciable amount of public criticism – obvious, vocal, and sometimes misplaced.

The British press so decried the short Lee-Enfield rifle (SMLE) that the authorities would have replaced it with a much clumsier Mauser derivative had not the First World War intervened. The US M1 Garand worked so poorly on its public debut that it was almost immediately withdrawn for alteration; the M16 (ArmaLite) was the butt of much criticism after apparently unacceptable combat showing in Vietnam. Even the Russians were so uncertain of the Kalashnikov *Avtomat* that they ordered the much more conventional SKS into series production in case the more radical concept should fail.

But the SMLE, the Garand, the M16 and the AK are now all regarded as runaway successes. One reason was that the authorities ignored public pressure and the much-heralded challenges of other guns sometimes proved to have more air than substance! In addition, history shows that it is very difficult to

The Kalashnikov has been made in many differing variants. This is a Yugoslavian M72 light machine-gun derivative.

challenge a well-established design, particularly if war is imminent. Thus the SMLE withstood the challenge of the P13 and P14 Mauser-type rifles, which were unarguably stronger (if more cumbersome), the Garand saw off the Johnson, and the M63 Stoner rifle failed to dislodge the M16 – both, ironically, designed by Gene Stoner. All three of these situations was influenced by war, the existence of manufacturing facilities in full production being an overwhelming argument in favour of maintaining status quo. There can be little doubt that the British were right to focus on the SMLE when the First World War began and the US Army was right to reject the Johnson in favour of the Garand so soon before the attack on Pearl Harbor. The case for the M16/M16A1 series was rather less obvious, even though the Vietnam war

was underway, and there were many in the US Army hierarchy who wanted to reintroduce the 7.62mm M14. The deciding factor was the US governmental reluctance to reverse the increasing reliance placed on commercial operations. Instead of abandoning the ArmaLite series, which would have meant reactivating machinery that had effectively been mothballed (it had soon been sold to Taiwan), the solution was to solve the problems as they arose and employ additional contractors to meet demand.

However, there have been instances where public opinion was unable to influence decisions taken at government level, even when these decisions were wrong. Among the worst cases is the Canadian Ross rifle, adopted in 1903, which was potentially dangerous to its firers. Early reports of serious injuries and

even a fatality or two failed to ring alarm bells in the highest circles, where a misguided sense of civic pride, the 'Old Country' aristocratic connections of the inventor and the autocratic tendencies of the Minister of War kept the Ross in service until it failed abjectly in the mud of Flanders during the First World War and was replaced by the short Lee-Enfield.

Ironically, the perfected Ross was incredibly strong and only a couple of comparatively minor design and manufacture flaws caused its rapid demise. But the greatest irony was that, in spite of the deaths and injuries that could be attributed to the rifle, Sir Charles Ross was rewarded with a $3 million pay-out when the Canadians sequestered the Ross Rifle Company factory! Another example of governmental blindness is provided by the problems encountered by the privately financed Berthier rifle in displacing the archaic but government-sponsored Lebel in French infantry service, and in the development of the Mle 1905 (Puteaux) and Mle 1907 (Saint-Étienne) machine-guns in France prior to the First World War. These machine-guns were adaptations of the Hotchkiss, a sturdy design that had won praise from the participants in the Russo-Japanese War of 1904–5, but were doomed to be as bad as the parent had been good. The French designers tinkered with the operating system to such little effect that the Puteaux was withdrawn to 'fortress defence' almost as soon as it had been introduced (a certain sign that it was a dismal failure) and the Saint-Étienne, though it served throughout the First World War, had superfluous changes made in its action.

These examples are historical, and it is often claimed that the same problems cannot affect weapons made of the latest materials on computer-controlled machinery. That they can is shown in the case of the British 5.56mm Individual Weapon (IW) and Light Support Weapon (LSW), developed in the early 1970s, introduced publicly as long ago as 1976, but a litany of disaster since mass production began. The 20,000 LSWs have

been withdrawn for scrapping (allowing the Bren Gun, a 1930s adoption, to reappear from store) and it seems highly likely that the rifles must inevitably follow if political courage is great enough. It can be argued, of course, that the faults reported from the Gulf War, peacekeeping duties in the Balkans and brushfire wars in places such as Sierra Leone are simply due to poor manufacture. If true, this is more a condemnation of British engineering than inherent design flaws. But once again, there is an unappreciated political dimension.

The original rifle was chambered for the 4.85mm cartridge, designed in Britain, but this was rejected in the course of NATO standardisation trials in favour of the American 5.56mm pattern.

Pressure brought to bear by the USA undoubtedly influenced other NATO representatives and, in retrospect, it seems naive of the British to have believed that the competition would be fair: once again, the existence of manufacturing facilities was enough to outweigh whatever intrinsic merits the 4.85mm round offered. With the decision taken, the British revised the rifle to accept the existing 5.56x45 round. Superficially, this seems an obvious course to take. But there are adverse precedents, where guns that worked with one particular cartridge failed when altered. Of course, this applies largely to automatic weapons such as the 8x51R and .30-06 CSRG (Chauchat) light machine-gun of the First World War era, as the US .30 M1917 Enfield rifle was just as efficient as its British .303 P14 prototype.

Reworking the XL64 and its derivatives for the 5.56mm cartridge should have been comparatively easy, but the different pressure/time characteristics of the cartridges disturbed the critical movement of the bolt mechanism. There are other instances of this happening; both FN-Herstal SA and SIG attempted to scale down guns that had worked well with 7.62x51 ammunition to handle 5.56x45, but both projects (the CAL and the SG530 respectively) were failures.

The British L86A1 Light Support Weapon, now withdrawn from service.

Modern firearms, like this Minimi light machine-gun, have to function in adverse conditions.

It has been said on more than one occasion that the British should have scrapped the entire IW project after the NATO standardisation trials and returned to first principles. Unusually for Britain, where there is a long history of adopting guns designed by non-Britons, chauvinism then played its part: the army could not be seen to buy another non-British design! The irony is that this could still happen if the L85A1 continues to perform badly.

The perils of small-arms design have been mentioned at length and may not seem relevant to the needs of specialised forces. Yet they are much more relevant than may seem. Demands made on the weaponry of the twenty-first century are far greater than they were even 30 years ago. This is partly due to the proliferation of specialist police SWAT and tactical firearms units and to the belated recognition by even the largest armies that the modern soldier is not the cannon-fodder he once was.

There was a time when the primary goals of a military weapon designer were strength and simplicity. Even the most ignorant recruit had to be able to master a gun quickly and an infantry rifle, for example, had to survive being repeatedly slammed butt-downward on the parade ground. Sights had to survive the ill-treatment to be encountered on field service and the barrels and fore-ends needed sufficient strength to anchor a bayonet thrust without breaking. Consequently, whatever their detail differences may have been, bolt-action infantry rifles almost always took similar form. The same was broadly true of machine-guns and infantry-support weapons.

One of the major changes was concerned more with manufacture than design. The advent of metal stamping and spot-welding, the development of lightweight alloys and plastics and the perfection of research methods allowed a step forward to be taken. Firearms issued during the Korean War would not have been unfamiliar to the participants in the First World War 40 years earlier, but one of the greatest changes has since been the universal issue of automatic weapons to the rank and file, acknowledging partly that individuals can now be trusted with more sophisticated equipment and partly that the ammunition-supply problems that so obsessed quartermasters have been conquered. It also reflects a fundamental change in warfare, away from the titanic set-piece confrontations of the first half of the twentieth century to the short, sharp, high-tech conflicts of the second half. These have seen the subjugation of the basic infantry weapon to helicopter gunships, missiles and laser-guided bombs. Thus the strength of armies has steadily declined, but, conversely, the standards of education have improved. Better-educated troops make better use of weapons, or at least so the theory runs, and this promotes the introduction of weapons that are technically superior to their antecedents.

But is this generalisation true? It undoubtedly contains elements of truth, yet there is another factor to consider: the influence of the arms manufacturers themselves. The supply of infantry rifles to the US Army, for example, represents a tremendous amount of work and (potentially) immense profits. The quantities involved can be enormous: contracts placed with Colt for 836,810 guns were valued at $91.7 million. Consequently, huge amounts of political lobbying – and often sizable inducements or 'commission' – can play a part in success. And it is very difficult to sustain success from one decade to the next: e.g., Colt's fortunes declined once large-scale procurement of the ArmaLite ceased, and Heckler & Koch

all but collapsed after support had been withdrawn from the G11 project.

Successful manufacturers are often best placed to ensure that their designs are accepted. These may not be the finest available, but the record of companies such as FN Herstal, Beretta, SIG and Heckler & Koch, and their contributions to employment, may be sufficient to sway governmental decisions. However, the ordnance business is cyclical and the last few decades have seen some of the best-known of all gunmaking businesses come close to failure. This is sometimes simply due to exceptionally successful designs coming to the end of their lives, which applies particularly to FN Herstal SA. The 7.62mm FAL and the 9mm GP-35 sold in huge quantities throughout the 1950s and 1960s and, even though the universal changeover to 5.56mm caught FN without a satisfactory rifle, the advent of the Minimi light machine-gun redressed the balance.

However, licensing of the Minimi elsewhere, and the limited markets found for the FNC, hit the company hard. A predatory bid by the French GIAT conglomerate was initially successful, but GIAT in turn encountered difficulties and FN was reconstituted – not the for the first time in its long and chequered history – as a smaller and more efficient unit. One of the casualties in a search for cost-

effectiveness was the superlative gun-engraving department, which caused a lot of ill-feeling in the Herstal area.

Heckler & Koch encountered problems when (with the 7.62mm G3 at the end of its life and the 5.56mm G41 enable to excite interest worldwide) the German government withdrew support from the caseless-cartridge G11 shortly before large-scale trials were to begin, blaming the unexpectedly high costs of reunification. H&K had already been acquired by British Aerospace, but was forced to cut back on its manufacturing capacity in Germany. However, the recent acceptance of the 5.56mm G36 and the 9mm P8 for service with the *Bundeswehr* looks likely to turn the adverse situation once more on its head.

Steyr-Mannlicher GmbH and SIG are each part of multi-strand trading groups, and still seem buoyant even though the large-scale contract to supply the Swiss Army with Stg 90 (SIG 550 series) assault rifles has now been completed. Another casualty has been Walther, which faced a similar problem to FN Herstal. The P1 (P38) and the PP/PPK series, all of which originated in the 1930s, were unable to compete with more effectual rivals. The introduction of the P88 was unable to boost the company's fortunes and the abject failure of the WA-2000 sniping rifle, in which huge sums had been invested,

Sporting derivatives of the M1 Carbine were made for many years. This Plainfield example has a sliding stock and an additional pistol grip.

provided a final nail in the coffin. Walther was acquired in 1993 by Umarex, a sporting-goods business, and has lost much of its identity. Only a few guns remain, though the introduction of the Walther P99 – successfully licensed to Smith & Wesson – may be a signal that things will improve.

Each failure, however, is usually offset by a success. One of the greatest rises has been that of the Glock pistol, designed by an otherwise unknown Austrian engineer, which caught the public imagination, quite mistakenly, as the 'undetectable gun'. The old adage that any publicity is good publicity ensured that the Glock was soon as firmly implanted in the public consciousness as longer-established handguns. Other successes have included Chartered Industries of Singapore with the SA-80 and SR-88 assault rifles and the Ultimax light machine-gun. Beretta, once owned in part

by FN Herstal SA, has also taken a leap forward. The adoption of the Mo. 92F pistol by the US armed forces (a controversial decision which history may show to be wrong) compensated for the end of work on the BM-59 series of modified 7.62x51 box-magazine Garands and the lack of enthusiasm being shown by the Italian army in the 5.56mm AR70. However, the Italian government has now adopted the AR70/90 for universal service and will place orders that may ultimately exceed a million guns.

Designing a combat firearm of any type is constrained by pre-determined parameters. For example, shortly before the Second World War began, the US Army Chief of Ordnance called for 'Light Rifle' submissions that met these criteria, and similar restrictions applied to the competition between the ArmaLite AR-15 and Winchester Light Automatc Rifle

(WLAR) in the late 1950s. Sometimes the manufacturers set the conditions themselves, but far more often an army has taken the lead. Even the revolutionary Heckler & Koch caseless-cartridge rifle was developed to satisfy a specification agreed by the *Bundeswehr* in the late 1960s.

Yet virtually all projects evolve within the same set of preconditions. Consequently, though individual requirements vary, the following 'ten tenets' apply to almost every individual case.

1. The gun must be strong and durable enough to withstand active service.
2. The gun must contain as few parts as possible.
3. The gun must be easy to make and economical in terms of materials.
4. The gun must be simple to operate and thus easily managed.
5. The gun must be as compact as possible ('envelope', 'footprint'), which usually means minimal overall length and weight.
6. The gun must handle well.
7. The gun must not jam in operation.
8. The gun must be easy to clean and simple to maintain.
9. The gun must be accurate, sufficiently powerful and offer sufficient range.
10. The gun must carry as much ammunition as possible in its magazine.

These categories are used as benchmarks in each class of gun. However, a rider to all these may be summarised as 'commensurate with the intended role'. Clearly, a handgun and a heavy machine-gun fulfil radically different roles, yet the basic desiderata remain the same. Each must be reliable and jam-free. Each must be as small and light as possible, but strong enough to survive rigorous combat. Maintenance must not be problematical, particularly where basic cleaning is concerned. And key parts must not break under duress.

Simplicity in any weapon is desirable, but not if it is taken to such extremes that function is impaired. However, though the simplicity of prototypes has often been the feature that commends them to military authorities, there is a tendency for trials boards to suggest additions, which bring with them penalties in the form of weight and unnecessary complexity. The ArmaLite R-15, in its original form, was a simpler gun than the M16; the M16, in turn was simpler than the supposedly improved M16A1 (which had a superfluous bolt-closing device); and the M16A1 was lighter and less complicated than the M16A2, which has a much heavier barrel. Consequently, a rifle than once weighed only a little over 6lb loaded now weighs 9lb. Soviet designers included a rate-reducing mechanism in the AKM –

was it worth the effort? – and even the original wartime German MP 43 assault rifle was modified by the addition of a bayonet lug and a grenade launcher before production began.

Unfortunately, many of the ten primary criteria listed above are conflicting instead of complementary and almost all weapons are compromises. This is particularly true where power and weight are concerned, as an increase in one is almost always accompanied by an increase in the other. Several very promising weapons have failed largely because they were, or were perceived to be, much too lightly built, including the Beardmore-Farquhar light machine-gun, the Soviet Simonov automatic rifle (AVS) and the Stoner 63/63A1 rifles.

Interest in small-calibre, high-velocity cartridges has nineteenth-century roots, when experimenters such as Hebler produced a variety of innovative bullet designs. Some had lightweight cores – one of Hebler's was essentially an open tube – and others simply reduced bullet diameter in pursuit of better sectional density and better 'carrying properties'. A more conventional Hebler cartridge was chambered in an experimental Krnka carbine, first tested in 1892, which was only two-thirds the weight of the infantry rifles of the day; like the rifle, the cartridge was smaller and

lighter than rival designs, yet offered comparable ballistics.

The US Navy briefly adopted a .236 (6mm) Lee straight-pull magazine rifle in 1895, but the project was a failure and a .30 cartridge was readopted with the Springfield rifle in 1903. Yet others persisted in questioning the traditional view that each new cartridge had to be larger than its predecessors and, in particular, more powerful than the ammunition used by neighbouring armies. This led to a form of arms race, but a desire for simplicity, a limit on the weight of infantry rifles (in practice, about 10lb with bayonet and loaded magazine) and the amount of recoil that could be accepted by the average soldier, led to a peak typified by the US .30-06 or 7.62x63mm rimless round. Few universal-issue rifle cartridges have offered greater power than this, though the Swedish Army did chamber a few Mauser rifles for an 8x63 machine-gun cartridge.

Experience in the First World War, during which much of the fighting took place within a grenade-throw of the enemy, led observers to question whether the rank and file needed weapons that were effective at distances measured in thousands of yards. Few men could aim well enough to guarantee a hit at even a few hundred yards, hindered by the coarseness and proven inaccuracy of their sights; ammunition was heavy and the guns themselves were cumbersome.

The introduction of the first Villar-Perosa and Bergmann submachine guns, which chambered conventional pistol ammunition, and the advent of the Pedersen Device, which fired a cartridge of roughly comparable power to the 9mm Parabellum, typified a new approach. The Germans are now normally credited with the development of the intermediate cartridge, but much of the pioneering work was done in Switzerland in the 1920s and it could be argued that the first true assault rifle was the Russian AVF of 1916. Designed by Vasiliy Fedorov, this chambered the low-power Japanese 6.5x50 semi-rimmed cartridge instead of the awkward and much more powerful 7.62x54R pattern.

Another departure from the norm was the acceptance of the US .30 M1 Carbine in 1941. This fired a cartridge that was midway in power between handgun and rifle ammunition and was specifically intended to arm men whose combat duties would be minimal. Eventually more than 6 million were made and, though most 'arms experts' roundly condemned it, the M1 was surprisingly successful on the

The FN Five-seveN® pistol and P90®
personal-defence weapon typify the current
generation of small arms.

battlefield. Many soldiers simply saw the M1 as a replacement for the .45 M1911A1 pistol, which had neither the range nor the accuracy to be an adequate self-defence at much other than point-blank range.

Arguments about cartridge power continued to rage. The 'Big Bore' school of US Army officers, having successfully forced the rejection of a .276 cartridge in the 1930s, insisted that NATO adopt the .30 T65 cartridge in the early 1950s, at a time when countries such as Britain were looking at something less traditional. It also resisted the move from the 7.62x51 NATO round, as the T65 had become, to the 5.56/.223 of the ArmaLite. The Spanish CETME rifle – initially chambering a 7.9x40 cartridge – was also revised for 7.62x51, leaving only the USSR firmly wedded to the concept of an assault rifle firing an intermediate cartridge. Experience with 5.56mm ammunition captured in Vietnam eventually persuaded the Soviets to move from the original 7.62x39 M43 cartridge to the 5.45x39 M74 round, but experimentation is *still* underway throughout the world.

FN Herstal SA has developed a 5.7x28 cartridge that can be chambered in both a pistol and a 'personal weapon' (basically a light automatic carbine) and Heckler & Koch, having experimented in the 1970s with a 4.5mm cartridge, are now touting a 4.6x30 design. Most of the experiments are aimed at providing multi-purpose weapons for non-combatants, but at the risk of complicating ammunition supply unless a wholesale change of direction is possible.

Standardising cartridges is laudable and the ideal situation is that every weapon, from handgun to heavy support machine-gun, should fire identical ammunition. This is clearly impossible, but efficient ammunition supply can be a key to battlefield mastery and a proliferation of cartridges is a serious logistical error. A divide has already been created between the adoption of small-calibre infantry weapons (5.45mm, 5.56mm) and the need to provide long-range supporting fire, customarily from weapons chambering the 7.62x51 or 7.62x54R cartridges. There are those who still champion the idea of a universal cartridge, perhaps midway between the 5.56x45 and 7.62x51 rounds, but the ideas are not taking hold. The ultimate answer is most probably the development of effectual caseless-cartridge ammunition.

Traditionally, successful machine-guns such as the Maxim were 'over-engineered', robust and in many respects much too sturdy for their role. This imbalance was challenged by many inventors from the late nineteenth century onward, but generally successfully defended by the military. However, manufacturing technology has improved so dramatically since the 1940s that the situation has now changed. Pioneered by the Germans during the Second World War, stamping, pressing, spot-welding and associated techniques have finally proved that form in the guise of mirror-polished surface finish – once indispensable in a military firearm – is not essential to function. This the Russians have known since the Revolution and many of the small arms produced in desperation in Germany during the last days of the Second World War worked just as well as their finely finished predecessors.

The most obvious advance has been in plastics, where long-term experimentation has provided material that is, quite literally, stronger than steel. An attractive feature of modern polymers is the ease with which they can be moulded into complex shapes, with none of the internal stresses that so often characterise metallic equivalents.

We are not yet in the era of the all-plastic 'undetectable gun' (not even the Glock pistol), owing to the need for metal springs and a metal barrel, but most observers predict that this will become a reality within 20 years. Plastic has now almost exclusively replaced wood grips and is already forming large parts of the receivers of many of the latest generation

A 5.56mm Steyr AUG equipped with a Pilkington Kite electro-optical sight.

of small arms. Barrels, bolts and breech blocks are still metal and so, too, are the rails on which the blocks slide. But it can only be a matter of time before even these parts are replaced.

However, synthetic components have a major drawback. Small-scale manufacture is often still undertaken by traditional means, using traditional gunsmithing materials. This is cost-effective largely because of the exceptional 'first cost' of the tooling and dies necessary to provide complex injection-moulded components. This can only be repaid by lengthy production runs, keeping the unit cost to acceptable levels, and in turn restricts the use of synthetic materials to the leading mass-market manufacturers.

Another area in which changes are sure to be made concerns ammunition. Though the Heckler & Koch/Dynamit Nobel cooperative failed to persuade the German government to adopt the G11 rifle and its caseless cartridge (the goal of inventors since Walter Hunt's Volitional Ball of 1848), progress was good enough to show that the concept would work once the inevitable teething troubles had been overcome. An effectual caseless-cartridge sporting rifle is already being marketed in Europe.

Trends in weapon design
The design of small arms, at least since the 1960s, has been complicated by ever-increasing demands. The traditional view of the infantryman as mindless, able only to understand the simplest equipment, has given way to an appreciation of the value of specialist training. This is partly due to improvements in education, partly to the influence of technology on warfare and partly to a reduction in the strength of armed forces that in turn places a premium on the skills of the individual.

Another factor to consider is the effect of changing patterns of warfare in the second half of the twentieth century; in the continued rise of specialist anti-terrorist units; and in the growth of police SWAT or tactical firearms units. The differences are obvious: armed forces must be equipped to fight in a variety of theatres, from cities and suburbs to deserts and wide-open plains; paramilitary and gendarmerie forces can be faced with a variety of situations, urban and rural; and police forces customarily operate within built-up areas.

An army has the least flexibility, owing to a need for standardised weapons, whereas, conversely, individual police forces are effectively at liberty to purchase whatever weapons meet their own peculiar circumstances. Consequently, there has been much more variety among the weapons of police marksmen, for example, than military snipers. The trends are not now as obvious as they were 20 years ago, but this merely reflects the ever-increasing stranglehold of the big gunmaking businesses and a move towards centralising control of police units.

Dimensions and performance data have been taken, where possible, from official handbooks and literature produced by the manufacturers. However, as this material is not always comprehensive, information (and conversions of dimensions) have occasionally been added. These 'unofficial' alterations are indicated with an asterisk (*); all other figures remain as originally written.

The Franchi SPAS-12 typifies current combat shotguns.

15

CONTENTS

HANDGUNS

The gun must be strong and durable enough to withstand active service. Virtually all modern handguns, even though their design may originate early in the twentieth century, meet these criteria. Once teething troubles that inevitably characterise the developmental stage have been overcome, comparatively few major failures are reported. Consequently, choice of a handgun is often dictated more by personal preference than the merits of individual designs. Revolvers are now customarily adapted from the Colt/Smith & Wesson swing-cylinder patterns and a desire for originality in the design of semi-automatic pistols has now largely given way to universal acceptance of modified forms of the Colt-Browning tipping-barrel lock – even by companies such as Walther and Heckler & Koch who had traditionally championed developments of their own.

The gun must contain as few parts as possible. Here there is some difference of opinion. Prior to the 1960s, the trend, particularly in military weapons, was to reduce the number of parts to the minimum. However, the belated influence of pre-1945 double-action guns such as the Walther *Polizei-Pistole*, the Mauser HSc and the Sauer Model 38 has created additional complexity in the trigger and safety systems. Though there is no doubt that these additions refine the performance of handguns – in particular, by removing the danger of accidental firing – there are those who are still of the opinion that a reversion to simplicity and the provision of better training is preferable.

The gun must be easy to make and economical in terms of materials. As explained above, there now two basic classes of handgun: those that are still made by traditional gunsmithing methods, albeit mechanised, and those that are designed to make use of the latest materials and manufacturing techniques. The first group contains most of the revolvers and also pistols such as the legion of M1911-type Colt-Browning derivatives. The latter includes guns such as the Glock, the Heckler & Koch USP/P8 series and the Walther P99, all of which embody a high proportion of synthetic parts. Guns such as the SIG-Sauers and the Rugers often represent an intermediate stage, made of modern materials by conventional metalworking techniques.

There is little doubt that the most modern designs are designed for a particular lifespan, a form of planned obsolescence, and undoubtedly lack the long-term durability of the original US Army M1911 and M1911A1 Colt-Brownings, which could, and indeed did, remain in service for decades. A different question is posed by the ageing of ultra-modern synthetic materials, an unknown quantity that, thanks to prolonged exposure to ultraviolet light or a breakdown of a stabiliser, may ultimately prevent guns lasting as long as predicted.

The gun must be simple to operate and thus easily managed. The addition of double-action triggers, ambidextrous (i.e., duplicated) controls and a multiplicity of safety systems has added greatly to the complexity of the handgun. Though the first generation of double-action guns has given way to refined designs, the problems still remain. There is an adage that the chance of breakage is directly proportional to an increase in features. Consequently, there are still a few experienced operatives championing the mechanical revolver, which, except for the incorporation of a transfer bar safety system, does not need to be fitted with the refinements of a modern semi-automatic pistol.

The gun must be as compact as possible. The design of handguns has changed appreciably in the last 30 years. There was a time when military pistols were large and comparatively cumbersome, often 8.5–9in (216–227mm) long. The current trend, accepting that the handgun is a short-range weapon, is to much more compact weapons closer to 6–8in overall. The length of the Glock 17 and the Heckler & Koch P7 are 186mm (7.32in) and 171mm (6.73in) respectively. The trends are obvious in the transition of the SIG-Sauer P220 (adopted in Switzerland in 1975) to the current P239, the reduction in length amounting to 26mm (1.02in). The US Army adopted the Beretta 92F in 1989, but this now seems a cumbersome gun – scarcely surprising, perhaps, as it dates from 1951 in its original guise. Beretta has accepted that the Model 92 is unwieldy, producing a series of compact derivatives, and FN Herstal (now committed to the Five-seveN®) followed a similar route with the FN-Browning GP-35 and BDA series.

The gun must handle well. The qualities of a handgun must remain subjective opinion. Praise has traditionally been given to the Luger and pistols like it, owing to the way they lie in the hand. The Luger, particularly in its 12cm-barrelled form, acts like an extension of the hand; point at a target as if with the index finger, and the gun unerringly follows. However, the magazine is raked too greatly to feed ammunition efficiently and the lightweight barrel does not facilitate a return to the target after each shot. Consequently, not only are the grips of almost all modern pistols squarer to the bore, but weight has been redistributed so that the centre of gravity lies as far forward of the trigger finger as possible. The same is true of revolvers, which, excepting slim-butt designs, often lie better in the hand than the pistols. The easiest way of rebalancing a revolver is to add a heavy barrel or extend the ejector-rod shroud to the muzzle to act as a weight.

The gun must not jam in operation.

Evidence from the trials such as the US JSSAP series suggests that modern handguns are no more efficient than the best pre-1939 examples. Revolvers of reputable origins have always been reliable, being subject to purely mechanical failure, whereas the effectiveness of semi-automatic pistols depends on the quality of their ammunition. The advent of double-action trigger systems has allowed pistols a 'second strike' capability, which may often fire a recalcitrant cartridge, but does not remove the perennial objection to auto-loading even though modern manufacturing technology ensures that defective cartridges are exceptionally rare.

The gun must be easy to clean and simple to maintain. Most modern handguns field-strip easily and can be cleaned with little trouble, but breakages in the trigger or safety systems can be difficult to repair.

The gun must be accurate, sufficiently powerful and offer sufficient range. Though long-range pistol shooting has many devotees, most military and police authorities now accept that the handgun has no real use other than ultra-short-range personal defence – or, suitably silenced, as an assassin's weapon. Submachine-guns such as the Heckler & Koch MP5 are usually preferred owing to the greater control offered by their weight. However, there are still those that insist that if a handgun is to be carried, it should be as powerful as possible to offer the greatest stopping power. This has led to an upsurge of interest in .45 ACP, which many US

special forces officers consider essential, and to new 'supra-9mm' cartridges such as 10mm and .40 S&W. A contrary opinion holds that as powerful handguns are not only difficult to control but also need a rigidly locked breech, most purposes can be served with compact double-action blowback pistols such as the 9mm Beretta 80 series or the ČZ 83. Neither case has ever been conclusively proven.

The gun must carry as much ammunition as possible. This is a perennial argument, dating from the widespread introduction of the 9mm GP-35 during the Second World War, when its magazine capacity – thirteen rounds – came as a revelation to Germans used to eight in a Luger or a Walther P38, and to Britons accustomed to six in a Webley revolver. However, the increase in capacity can only be achieved with a staggered- or two-column magazine, in turn leading to a thick grip that is not universally popular. The advent of 10mm and .40 rounds has exacerbated problems traditionally encountered even with 9x19 (9mm Parabellum) ammunition and most manufacturers are now offering single-row magazine options. High-capacity magazines have never been suited to the .45 ACP, owing to the large external diameter of the case, though attempts have been made.

Details of only a few typical designs are given here. Additional information can be found in another Greenhill Military Manual – Ian Hogg, *Small Arms: Pistols and Rifles* (2001).

Revolvers

The popularity of the revolver has declined greatly in recent years. Once almost universally issued to policemen, the 'wheel gun' has now been largely supplanted by semi-automatic pistols. Partly this reflects military usage, promoted as the boundaries between military, paramilitary and police forces gradually blur. But is also reflects the restrictions of a cylindrical magazine: limited capacity commensurate with a compact profile and reloading problems even when yoke-mounted.

Many modern service-type pistols offer double the magazine capacity of a revolver, and a detachable box magazine can be replenished simply by substituting a new one. Equally, compact pistols are flatter and much more easily concealed than even the shortest small-frame revolver. So why do revolvers survive? Their champions point to safety and reliability and often also to the exemplary handling qualities of the best-balanced examples.

A double-action revolver is usually simpler mechanically than a double-action pistol, particularly as the latter normally offers duplicated ambidextrous controls and additional de-cocking features. Mechanical systems do not rely on the efficiency of a cartridge to function and can almost always fire a second shot in safety. A misfire in a pistol, especially if a cartridge jams in the chamber, is customarily much more difficult to clear. However, the material and design of critical components in the firing mechanism of a revolver (especially the relationship between the sear and the trigger lever) must be good enough to ensure long-term reliability.

The best revolvers are those that embody transfer-bar safety systems, which have been particularly evident since the Gun Control Act of 1968 became law in the USA; transfer bars block the passage of the hammer to the striker, preventing the revolver firing except in the final stages of a deliberate trigger pull, and remove the need for an additional mechanical safety. Few modern multi-function pistols are as simple or reliable, owing to the multiplicity of components and, as a hammer can be seen or felt at all times, the revolver firer can easily check on the state of cocking.

These advantages are often claimed to be more illusory than real and virtually all practical pistol-shooting prizes are now being won with modern semi-automatic pistols. However, the speed-shooting records are almost all held with revolver.

Guns of this type, which are made worldwide by a variety of manufacturers, have been popular for self-defence. This Brazilian example, a copy of the Smith & Wesson, relies on a conventional yoke-mounted cylinder and a double-action lock mechanism. The gun illustrated – with an ultra-short barrel – has a conventional spurred hammer that allows deliberate (single-action) fire when practicable. The front sight blade takes the form of a ramp, ribbed to reduce the effect of reflections and tapered to reduce the chances of snagging clothing or a holster.

The Taurus Model 85 may be obtained with an alloy or steel frame and a variety of grips, the featured example having tapered walnut stocks. These are not particularly efficient, especially in adverse conditions when moisture, oil or grease will make them difficult to hold; in addition, they do not fill the hand well enough to prevent the gun slipping upward out of the palm during firing. Chequering would undoubtedly improve performance.

Made by Forjas Taurus SA, Porto Alegre-RS, Brazil

Specification Double-action personal-defence revolver
Data from a manufacturer's leaflet, dated 1990
Calibre .38
Cartridge .38 Special, rimmed
Operation Manual, single shot only
Locking system Latch on left side of frame

Length 175mm (6.90in*)
Weight 595g (21.0oz*), empty, alloy frame
Barrel 50mm (1.97in*), 6 grooves, right-hand twist
Magazine 5-chamber rotating cylinder
Muzzle velocity 229m/sec* (750ft/sec*) with ball ammunition

The Taurus Model 85 revolver.

Manurhin MR Special Police F1 France

Manurhin remains best known for the MR-73 revolver, but concerns that this gun was too expensive to appeal to police forces led to the creation of the RMR (Revolver Manurhin-Ruger), which was basically a Ruger Service Six frame mated with an MR-73 cylinder/barrel unit. In 1984, however, after problems with the licence, the cooperative venture was abandoned. Manurhin then produced the MR SP-1, which, though retaining Ruger-like lines, reverted to the detachable-sideplate frame of the MR-73. Production ceased when the revolver-making business was sold to FN Herstal SA in 1989 and then transferred to the newly formed Browning-France SA.

This particular gun, with a 75mm barrel, has a short ramped front sight, tapered to reduce snagging to a minimum and a double-action lock mechanism that offers the possibility of a rapid double-action first shot or, if time permits, deliberate single-action fire, achieved by thumb-cocking the hammer. The wood butt has chequered panels on each side – too small to be useful, perhaps – but the flared heel permits a firmer grip than the rounded design of the Taurus Model 85.

The RMR1 shows its Ruger ancestry most obviously in the shape of the frame.

Made by Manurhin–Manufacture de Machines du Haut Rhin (Matra-Manurhin Défense), Mulhouse-Bourtzwiller, France
Specification Double-action personal-defence revolver

Data from Ian Hogg, *The Greenhill Military Small Arms Data Book* (1999)
Calibre .357
Cartridge .357 Magnum, rimmed
Operation Manual, single shot only
Locking system Latch on left side of frame
Length 207mm (8.15in*)
Weight 950g (33.51oz*), empty
Barrel 75mm (2.95in*), 6 grooves, right-hand twist
Magazine 6-chamber rotating cylinder
Muzzle velocity 427m/sec* (1400ft/sec*) with ball ammunition

Franchi RF-83 Italy

The Franchi is basically a copy of Colt practice, relying on a backward pull on the cylinder shield on the rear left side of the frame to release the cylinder yoke. Made in a variety of patterns, ranging from 'Extra Small' (described here) to 'Super Target' with a heavy 15cm (5.9in) barrel and adjustable sights, it has conventional double-action lockwork, incorporating a transfer bar safety system, and a hammer with a low spur. The gun shown is a short-barrelled personal-defence weapon, with rudimentary sights. The ramped front sight and the ejector-rod shroud are intended to reduce the chance of snagging clothing or a holster during a draw.

This particular gun has wooden grips, too smooth to give an adequate grasp in adverse conditions. It also offers an electroless satin nickel finish, which resists corrosion better than conventionally blued steel. Plated finishes (nickel or chrome) were once popular, but tended to flake and often wore rapidly to expose the base metal. Stainless steel is now preferred wherever possible, but is appreciably more expensive than traditional blued steel and has yet to become truly universal.

Made by Luigi Franchi SpA, Divisione Sistemi Difensivi, Fornaci/Brescia, Italy
Specification Double-action personal-defence revolver
Data from manufacturer's leaflet, *RF 83 cal. 38 Special* (c. 1986)
Calibre .38
Cartridge .38 Special, rimmed
Operation Manual, single shot only

Locking system Latch on left side of frame
Length 197mm* (7.75in*)
Weight 630g (22.2oz*), empty
Barrel 50mm (1.97in*), 6 grooves, right-hand twist
Magazine 6-chamber rotating cylinder
Muzzle velocity 229m/sec* (750ft/sec*) with ball ammunition

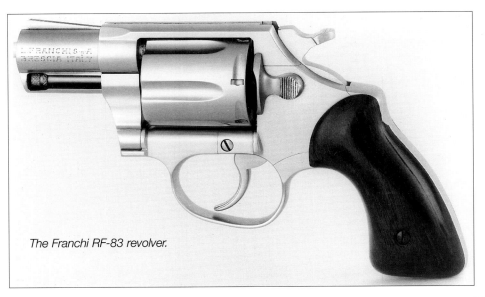

The Franchi RF-83 revolver.

Introduced in the 1970s by the Charter Arms Corporation, based on patents granted to Douglas McClenahan, this otherwise conventional double-action revolver is distinguished by a short (55°) hammer fall and an unbreakable copper/beryllium inertia-type firing pin set into the frame. The cylinder is mounted on a yoke, which can be swung out to the left once the catch on the left side of the frame behind the cylinder has been pressed.

Chambering the Law Enforcement Bulldog for the powerful .44 Special cartridge, though this restricts cylinder capacity, improved 'stopping power' in what is otherwise a compact, lightweight weapon. The gun illustrated, which has a 3in (76mm) barrel discontinued in favour of 2.5in (63mm) in 1988, has a spurless 'pocket hammer' designed to be thumb-cocked when necessary – with some difficulty! – and a hand-filling wraparound neoprene grip. The ramped front sight is perhaps too sharply contoured to prevent snagging and the head of the ejector rod could perhaps be shrouded, but the Bulldog has proved a popular off-duty weapon with policemen throughout North America.

Made by Charco, Inc., Ansonia, Connecticut, USA (formerly Charter Arms Corporation, Stratford, Connecticut)
Specification Double-action personal-defence revolver
Data from Ian Hogg and John Weeks, *Pistols of the World* (first edition, 1992)
Calibre .44
Cartridge .44 S&W Special, rimmed

Operation Manual, single shot only
Locking system Latch on left side of frame
Length 191mm (7.50in)
Weight 539g (19.0oz), empty
Barrel 76mm (3in), 6 grooves, right-hand twist
Magazine 5-chamber rotating cylinder
Muzzle velocity 232m/sec* (760ft/sec) with ball ammunition

A Charco (Charter Arms) Law Enforcement Bulldog revolver, with its 'pocket hammer'.

Ruger GP-100

Introduced in 1986, the Ruger GP series replaced the Service Six and Security Six revolvers. Though sharing an essentially similar yoke-mounted cylinder and double-action lockwork, complete with transfer bar, the GP offers a full-length ejector-rod shroud beneath the barrel and grips consisting of Goncalo Alves wood panels set in neoprene cushions. Ruger claims that this improves performance and there can be no doubt that the additional under-barrel weight (provided by the shroud) gives the muzzle heaviness preferred for snap-shooting.

The top rib is ribbed to reduce the effects of glare. The blued-finish gun shown has a 4in barrel and adjustable sights, which are useful unless the gun is needed for fast-draw personal defence – in which case a shorter barrel and fixed sights are preferable.

The Ruger GP-100 is distinguished by the full-length ejector shroud and the design of the grip.

Made by Sturm, Ruger & Co. Inc., Southport, Connecticut, and Prescott, Arizona, USA
Specification Double-action general-purpose revolver
Data from Ian Hogg and John Weeks, *Pistols of the World* (first edition, 1992)
Calibre .357
Cartridge .357 Magnum, rimmed
Operation Manual, single shot only

Locking system Latch on left side of frame
Length 239mm (9.4in)
Weight 1160g (41.0oz), empty
Barrel 102mm (4.0in), 6 grooves, right-hand twist
Magazine 6-chamber rotating cylinder
Muzzle velocity 427m/sec* (1400ft/sec) with ball ammunition

Smith & Wesson Model 624   USA

This snub-nosed revolver typifies the trend towards compact high-power personal-defence weapons, though chambering such a powerful cartridge in a gun weighing 36oz restricts it only to strong-handed firers.

The M624 is a classical stainless-steel design, with a yoke-mounted cylinder that can be swung sideways once the catch on the rear left side of the frame (behind the cylinder shield) has been pressed forward. The double-action lockwork incorporates a transfer-bar safety system, and the ejector-rod head

is protected by a full-length shroud. The gun illustrated – an example of the short-lived Lew Horton Special – has a short barrel and sturdy adjustable sights, which could be a liability in a fast-draw situation by snagging clothing. The rounded wooden grips are contoured to give an effective grip, though synthetic neoprene or similar alternatives would be better all-round performers in military or police service.

Made by Smith & Wesson, Inc., Springfield, Massachusetts, USA
Specification Double-action personal-defence revolver
Data from Ian Hogg, *The Greenhill Military Small Arms Data Book* (1999)
Calibre .44
Cartridge .44 Magnum, rimmed
Operation Manual, single shot only
Locking system Latch on left side of frame
Length 232mm* (9.13in)
Weight 1020g* (36.0oz), empty
Barrel 76mm* (3.0in), 5 grooves, right-hand twist
Magazine 6-chamber rotating cylinder
Muzzle velocity 448m/sec* (1470ft/sec) with ball ammunition

A snub-nose Smith & Wesson M624 revolver.

Semi-automatic pistols, traditional forms

These are the survivors of guns that originated, in some cases, prior to the First World War. They are often very sturdy, being made of traditional materials, and are rarely subject to operating problems – these have been overcome during production lives that may have extended over 60 years or more. However, the guns are often larger than the current generation of handguns, expensive to make and, excepting the FN-Browning GP-35, have magazine capacities restricted to no more than a couple of rounds more than a revolver.

Though several agencies still make the Colt-Browning M1911A1 Government Model in a variety of guises – including competition-shooting guns with extended barrels, muzzle brakes and stabilisers – these are rarely encountered in the hands of special forces.

The 9mm FN-Browning GP-35 Vigilant pistol.

One of the greatest of all handgun designs, this was patented by John Browning in the 1920s and had been perfected by 1929. However, production was delayed until the worst effects of the Depression had receded. Guns had been made for Belgium, China and elsewhere when the Second World War begun and were then supplied in quantity to the German Army, by the FN factory working under occupation, and copies made by John Inglis & Company in Toronto were supplied to the British, Canadians and Chinese. Work began again after the end of the war and by 1980 guns of this type had been issued to military and paramilitary forces in 60 countries.

The GP-35, also known as the High Power or HP, is comparatively simple, with an action locked by ribs on the top surface of the barrel engaging recesses cut in the slide. Recoil allows a cam-link to tip the barrel downward at the rear, breaking the lock and allowing the slide to reciprocate alone. A new cartridge is pushed forward into the chamber on the return stroke, the barrel is lifted until the lugs engage with the slide, the parts run back into battery and the gun is ready to be fired again. This simple system was pioneered prior to the First World War in the Colt-Brownings, culminating in the M1911 Government Model.

The GP-35 was the first service pistol to offer the large-capacity that is now commonplace on military weapons, achieved simply by staggering the cartridges. Thirteen rounds were far better than the six customarily offered by revolvers, or the eight rounds of guns such as the Luger or the Walther P38. The gun pictured is a Vigilant variant, with fixed sights, matt finish, injection-moulded synthetic grips and a lanyard ring on the butt heel.

However, by the 1980s, the Browning had been overtaken by modern designs such as the Glock, though even this relies on the same tipping-barrel operating system. FN could not hope to compete and production of the GP was greatly reduced, sufficient only to allow for limited military/paramilitary sales and the burgeoning collectors'/commercial market.

An attempt was made to introduce a double-action version, the HP DA, but the trigger mechanism proved to be too weak to succeed. This led to a purpose-designed double-action derivative, the BDA (Browning Double Action); offered in full-length, compact and 'pocket' versions, this appeared too late to challenge the Beretta 92 series and the Glock and had been abandoned by 1995 in favour of improved forms of the old single-action gun the Marks 2 and 3 – with ambidextrous controls and improved safety features.

Made by Fabrique Nationale d'Armes de Guerre and FN Herstal SA, Herstal-lèz-Liège, Belgium
Specification Semi-automatic pistol Data from Ian Hogg, *The Greenhill Military Small Arms Data Book* (1999)
Calibre 9mm
Cartridge 9x19 (9mm Parabellum), rimless
Operation Recoil, semi-automatic only
Locking system Modified Browning tipping barrel
Length 197mm (7.75in)
Weight 1000g (35.0oz) with empty magazine
Barrel 120mm (4.72in), 4 grooves, right-hand twist
Magazine 13-round detachable box
Muzzle velocity 350m/sec (1148ft/sec) with ball ammunition

Though superficially just another of the Browning tipping-barrel clones, this pistol has been unusually successful, particularly as its manufacturer was operating within the Soviet bloc when the original version, the ČZ-75, was introduced. Consequently, the initial sales were almost all exports.

Purchasers soon realised that the double-action ČZ-75, still made of traditional materials by traditional methods, represented excellent value. This was at least partly due to the design of the slide,

which was carried on rails machined inside the frame in the manner of the SIG SP47/8 (*Ordonnanzpistole* 49); like its Swiss predecessor, the ČZ has a reputation for good accuracy. It balances well in the hand, has a large-capacity magazine and an unobtrusive ring hammer allowing single-action fire.

The principal difference between the ČZ-75 and its successor, the ČZ-85, concerns the controls. The manual safety catch and the slide-stop found only on the left side of the ČZ-75 frame are duplicated on the ČZ-85 to provide ambidexterity. In addition, the front of the trigger-guard bow on the newer gun is squared and ribbed to provide a better two-handed grip. The ČZ-85 backsight can be adjusted latterly and changes made within the lockwork make the action smoother.

Still made in quantity in the Czech

Republic, the influential ČZ has been copied in Switzerland by ITM of Solothurn (now Sphinx Industries); in Italy, by Tanfoglio; and in Israel, where the Jericho 941 is little more than an adaptation of the Tanfoglio pistol with rapidly exchangeable 9mm Parabellum/.41 Action Express magazine, barrel and mainspring units. Guns will also be found with the marks of Springfield Armory of Geneseo, Illinois, but these are made in Europe.

Made by Ceská Zbrojovka, Uhersky Brod
Specification Semi-automatic pistol
  Data from Ian Hogg, *The Greenhill Military Small Arms Data Book* (1999)
Calibre 9mm
Cartridge 9x19 (9mm Parabellum), rimless
Operation Recoil, semi-automatic only
Locking system Modified Browning tipping barrel
Length 203mm (8in)
Weight 980g (35oz) with empty magazine
Barrel 120mm (4.72in), 6 grooves, right-hand twist
Magazine 15-round detachable box
Muzzle velocity 396m/sec (1300ft/sec) with ball ammunition

The 9mm Czech ČZ-85 double-action pistol.

Walther is renowned for the pre-war P38, used in large numbers by the *Wehrmacht*, and for its post-war reincarnation, the P1. These guns incorporated a locking system patented in the 1930s by Fritz Walther and Fritz Barthelmes, which relied on a pin floating in the frame to depress the locking-piece as the barrel and slide recoiled. The only idea to challenge the supremacy of the Browning-link and cam-finger depressors in recent years, it was too complicated to

The Walther P88 Compact embodies a variant of the Colt-Browning tipping-barrel action.

succeed when, in the cost-conscious 1970s, the German authorities began to look closely at their service weapons. Though the P1 was retained by the police in Berlin and limited interest was shown in the Walther P5, a modernised P1, most other forces opted for the P6 (SIG-Sauer P226) or the P7 (Heckler & Koch).

The obsolescence of the P1/P5 series coincided with a serious downturn in Walther's fortunes, owing partly to the unexpected death of Karl-Heinz Walther and a loss of its once pre-eminent market position to Heckler & Koch. The P88 (1989) was the first attempt to provide a modern military-style pistol, abandoning the Walther/Barthelmes lock in favour of a Browning-inspired cam finger. A de-cocking system was retained, with ambidextrous controls on the slide, but the P88 was still too traditionally made

and thus too expensive to succeed; the military and police markets had become dominated by uncertainty and also by a move towards largely synthetic designs, even though this meant accepting a form of planned obsolescence.

Though target-shooting versions of the P88 are still being made, the military-style guns, including the P88 Compact (introduced in 1992), have now been abandoned in favour of the P99.

Made by Carl Walther Sportwaffenfabrik GmbH, Ulm/Donau and Arnsberg, Germany
Specification Semi-automatic pistol
Data from manufacturer's literature dated October 1994
Calibre 9mm
Cartridge 9x19, rimless
Operation Recoil, semi-automatic only
Locking system Modified Browning tipping barrel
Length 181mm (7.13in*)
Weight 822g (29.0oz*) with empty magazine
Barrel 97mm (3.82in*), 6 grooves, right-hand twist
Magazine 14-round detachable box
Muzzle velocity 350m/sec* (1148ft/sec*) with ball ammunition

Beretta Model 84

Inspired by the success of the Walther *Polizei-Pistole* and the other German double-action personal-defence pistols introduced prior to 1945, this range of Italian-made uncomplicated blowbacks depends on the quality of construction for its success. The guns are offered in variants ranging from single-action target pistols and the 7.65mm Auto Model 81 to the Model 84, pictured here, chambering cartridges powerful enough to be a potent self-defence.

The double-action trigger mechanism and exposed hammer represent conventional design, with a manual safety lever and a slide-stop on the left side of the frame and a cross-bolt magazine catch behind the trigger-guard bow. However, the magazine is a staggered-row large-capacity design and the handling qualities are exemplary.

Though guns such as these are rarely encountered in front-line service, the Berettas and comparable designs (e.g., the ČZ-83) provide good back-up. Their compact dimensions and comparatively low-powered ammunition suit them ideally to close-range use. A variant has been made in comparatively small numbers by FN Herstal SA in Belgium, as the FN 140 DA. It may be distinguished from the Italian equivalents by its closed-top slide: the Beretta representatives display the characteristic barrel-exposing cutaway.

Made by Fabbrica d'Armi Pietro Beretta SpA, Gardone V.T. (Brescia), Italy
Specification Semi-automatic pistol
Data from Ian Hogg, *The Greenhill Military Small Arms Data Book* (1999)
Calibre 9mm

Cartridge 9x17 (9mm Short), rimless
Operation Blowback, semi-automatic only
Locking system None
Length 172mm (6.77in)
Weight 660g (23.0oz) with empty magazine
Barrel 97mm (3.82in), 6 grooves, right-hand twist
Magazine 13-round detachable box
Muzzle velocity 280m/sec (918ft/sec) with ball ammunition

The Beretta M84 personal-defence pistol chambered the 9mm Short cartridge. Note the staggered-column magazine.

Beretta Model 92F Compact   Italy

This owes its origins to the single-action Model 951 or Brigadier pistol, developed by Beretta shortly after the end of the Second World War and introduced commercially, after trials and tribulations, in the mid-1950s. Successful enough to be adopted by the Italian armed forces, the M951 embodied an adaptation of the Walther/Barthelmes pin-and-block locking system introduced in the Walther P38 – the only system to challenge the supremacy of the Browning-type tipping barrel since 1945.

However, the Beretta is weaker in the frame than the Walther, owing to a cutaway on the side of the magazine well and a few failures were reported in the earliest days. These were cured by improving metallurgy and redesigning the parts, though the theoretical weakness still remains.

The original pistol was replaced in 1976 by the Model 92, with a double-action trigger system, and then by the Model 92S, with a safety catch/de-cocking lever mounted on the slide instead of a simple safety catch on the frame. The Model 92SB, developed for the US JSSAP trials, had an ambidextrous safety catch on the slide and an automatic firing-pin safety mechanism and the magazine catch was moved from the heel of the butt to the frame behind the trigger.

The Beretta has proved to be exceptionally successful and has been adopted by a wide variety of military, paramilitary and police forces. It is larger and clumsier than the current generation of Glock and SIG-Sauer pistols, however.

The perfected Model 92FS, with ambidextrous controls, an extended magazine base, a swell-front grip and a ribbed straight-front trigger guard was adopted, somewhat controversially, by the US Army as the '9mm Pistol M9' and then, once a de-cocking lever had been added (M92G), by the French as the PA MAS-G1. Production in Gardone has been supplemented by the output of the Beretta USA factory in Accokeek, Maryland and by guns made under licence in France by the Manufacture d'Armes de Saint-Étienne, in Brazil by Forjas Taurus and in South Africa by Lyttleton Industries (now Vektor).

The illustration shows the shortened M92F Compact, with plastic grips; other variants include the Model 92D, self-cocking only; the M92DS, a 92D with the safety lever on the slide; the Model 92SB Compact; and the Model 92SB Type M with a single-row (eight rounds) magazine. The Model 98 and Model 99 were 7.65mm variants of the 92SB Compact and 92SB Type M respectively.

A Beretta Model 92-F Compact pistol, with ambidextrous de-cocking lever and magazine-release button.

Made by Fabbrica d'Armi Pietro Beretta SpA, Gardone V.T. (Brescia), Italy
Specification Semi-automatic pistol Data from Ian Hogg, *The Greenhill Military Small Arms Data Book* (1999)
Calibre 9mm
Cartridge 9x19, rimless
Operation Recoil, semi-automatic only
Locking system Modified Walther pin and block
Length 197mm (7.76in)
Weight 910g (32.0oz) with empty magazine
Barrel 109mm (4.29in), 6 grooves, right-hand twist
Magazine 13-round detachable box
Muzzle velocity 390m/sec (1280ft/sec) with ball ammunition

Desert Eagle

One of the most interesting handguns to see use with special forces, the Desert Eagle offers a long-range performance that few service pistols can match. Originally chambered for the .357 Magnum revolver cartridge, a rimmed round that seemed unsuitable for a semi-automatic pistol, the gun is gas operated. Part of the propellant gas is tapped from the muzzle to force the bolt back far enough for the camming action of a stud inside the slide, acting on a slot in the bolt, to rotate the latter far enough to break the lock with the barrel.

The Desert Eagle is large and cumbersome, but ideally suited to situations where a powerful and unusually accurate pistol must be used. Optical sights mounts can be clamped to the barrel, combat or target sights may be fitted and chamberings have ranged from the original .357 Magnum to .50 Action Express.

The Desert Eagle has often been condemned as too unwieldy to be successful, but is lighter than its bulk suggests. Its size is largely due to the necessity to slow the opening of the bolt until pressure in the chamber has dropped to a safe level. This is accomplished by tapping gas immediately ahead of the chamber, leading it forward to the muzzle and only then into the gas cylinder. One advantage of this construction lies in the fixed barrel, which results in better accuracy than a tipping-barrel gun.

Made by Israeli Military Industries (IMI), Ramat ha-Sharon, Israel

Specification Semi-automatic pistol
Data from Ian Hogg and John Weeks, *Pistols of the World* (first edition, 1992)
Calibre .357

Cartridge .357 Magnum, rimmed
Operation Gas, semi-automatic only
Locking system Lugs on the rotating bolt lock into the slide
Length 260mm (10.24in*)
Weight 1.715kg (60.5oz) with empty magazine
Barrel 150mm (5.91in), 6 grooves, right-hand twist
Magazine 9-round detachable box
Muzzle velocity 436m/sec* (1430ft/sec*) with ball ammunition

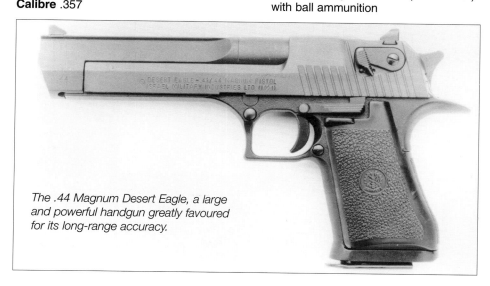

The .44 Magnum Desert Eagle, a large and powerful handgun greatly favoured for its long-range accuracy.

A variant of the legendary Colt-Browning Government Model pistol (M1911/M1911A1), introduced in 1987 for the then-new 10mm Norma or '10mm Auto' cartridge, this offers the virtues of its prototype: simplicity, durability and power. However, few concessions have been made to modernity, except for three-dot tritium sights: the single-column magazine remains, together with single-action trigger and the original manual safety catch/slide-stop assembly on the left side of the frame.

The barrel bush gives better support to the muzzle than the original, improving accuracy, and wraparound neoprene gives a better grip than the original walnut stocks. The hammer has a ring instead of a spur, and better sights are fitted, but the essence of the Delta Elite remains pure 1909-patent Browning! But there are many for whom nothing better than the original .45-calibre variant can be obtained.

Made by the Firearms Division, Colt Industries, Hartford, Connecticut, USA
Specification Semi-automatic pistol Data from a manufacturer's catalogue, dated 1989
Calibre 10mm
Cartridge 10x25 (10mm Norma), rimless
Operation Recoil, semi-automatic only

Locking system Browning tipping barrel
Length 213mm* (8.4in)
Weight 1090g* (38.5oz) with empty magazine
Barrel 127mm* (5.0in), 4 grooves, right-hand twist
Magazine 8-round detachable box
Muzzle velocity 351m/sec* (1150ft/sec) with ball ammunition

The 10mm-calibre Colt Delta Elite is just one of the many variants of the legendary Colt-Browning Government Model adopted in 1911.

Smith & Wesson Model 469

If the Colt-Browning represented the high point of US semi-automatic pistol design prior to 1945, then the Smith & Wessons are the apogee of the 1960s. Designed soon after the end of the Second World War by Joseph Norman, initially in single-action form, the basic design was eventually developed into an efficient double-action handgun handicapped only by the reluctance of the US police forces to move away from their tried-and-tested revolvers.

The gun shown (dating from 1985–8) represents one of the most compact of Smith & Wesson's offerings, with a short barrel and a spurless hammer which, though giving a clear indication of the cocking state, nonetheless makes single-action shooting impossible.

This particular gun has an ambidextrous safety catch/de-cocking lever on the slide, a slide-stop on the left side of the frame above the trigger and stippled Delrin grips.

The front and back straps are ribbed to improve grip, the sights are minimalistic, the magazine base is extended to improve grip and the front of the trigger guard has been squared to facilitate a two-handed shooting.

Made by Smith & Wesson, Inc., Springfield, Massachusetts, USA
Specification Semi-automatic pistol Data from Ian Hogg and John Weeks, *Pistols of the World* (first edition, 1992)
Calibre 9mm
Cartridge 9x19, rimless
Operation Recoil, semi-automatic only

Locking system Modified Browning tipping barrel
Length 175mm (6.90in*)
Weight 735g (25.9oz*) with empty magazine
Barrel 89mm (3.5in*), 6 grooves, right-hand twist
Magazine 12-round detachable box
Muzzle velocity 330m/sec* (1083ft/sec*) with ball ammunition

The Smith & Wesson M469, with a bobbed hammer.

Smith & Wesson Model 3904

An updated form of the original Model 39, made in 1989–91, this has a fixed barrel bushing, a safety catch/de-cocking lever on the slide and a double-action trigger system. The hammer has a bobbed tip, reducing snagging without compromising thumb-cocking, and the adjustable backsight is protected by sturdy wings. The grips on this gun are synthetic Delrin, with integrally moulded ribs on the straps, but wood can be obtained as an option. The sights, which can be fixed or adjustable, are three-dot tritium patterns.

Smith & Wesson pistols have sold in large numbers across the USA, though now challenged by guns such as the Ruger, the Glock and the Beretta 92 series, but the US Army service pistol, the M9, has never convinced police and paramilitary agencies of its merits.

Made by Smith & Wesson, Inc.,
    Springfield, Massachusetts, USA
Specification Semi-automatic pistol
    Data from Ian Hogg and John Weeks,
    Pistols of the World (first edition, 1992)
Calibre 9mm
Cartridge 9x19, rimless
Operation Recoil, semi-automatic only
Locking system Modified Browning
    tipping barrel
Length 191mm (7.52in*)
Weight 725g (25.6oz*) with empty
    magazine
Barrel 102mm (4.0in*), 6 grooves,
    right-hand twist
Magazine 8-round detachable box
Muzzle velocity 350m/sec* (1148ft/sec*)
    with ball ammunition

The Smith & Wesson M3904 has shrouded sights and the trigger guard squared to facilitate a two-hand grip.

Semi-automatic pistols, transitional designs

These link traditionally made pistols such as the Colt M1911A1 or the Walther P1 (P38) with modernistic designs such as the Glock. The incorporation of a profusion of stamped parts does not necessarily compromise their performance, though many trials have been more concerned with establishing a service life based on rounds fired than ultimate timescale.

For example, the 1979 JSSAP trials set the projected life at 10,000 rounds. It seems unlikely that many of these transitional pistols will still be serviceable in 50 years time.

SIG-Sauer P226

Switzerland/Germany

The 9mm SIG-Sauer P226.

Designed in Switzerland, but exported only with the cooperation of J.P. Sauer & Sohn GmbH, these pistols are essentially modernised Colt-Brownings. The principal difference concerns the locking system, which has become a squared barrel-block that rises through a port in the slide. When the gun fires, a shaped finger under the block acts on a transverse shoulder on the frame to tip the barrel downward, freeing the block from the slide and allowing the latter to reciprocate alone.

The slide is an investment casting and many of the minor parts, such as the trigger lever and the external controls, are stampings or pressings. The guns originally lacked ambidextrous controls, with the safety catch, de-cocking lever and the slide-stop on the left side of the frame and a cross-bolt magazine catch through the frame behind the trigger aperture. The sights are generally fixed, the hammer is a bobbed form resistant to snagging and the plastic grips wrap around the butt.

The original pistol, the P220 (*Ordonnanzpistole* 75 in Swiss service) has been superseded by the compact P225 and P226, the latter being developed in 1980 for the US JSSAP trials that led to the standardisation of the Beretta Model 92F, apparently on price. The guns are essentially similar, except that the P226 has an ambidextrous magazine release. The P220 and P225 all have eight-round, single-column magazines, a perceived gap in the range being filled with the P228 (9mm Parabellum, thirteen rounds) and P229 (.40 S&W, twelve rounds). Most guns have steel slides and aluminium alloy frames, though an 'SL' suffix indicates a stainless steel slide instead of the standard blued pattern.

Made by SIG–Schweizerische Industrie-Gesellschaft, Neuhausen/Rheinfalls, Switzerland

Specification Semi-automatic pistol
Data from Ian Hogg, *The Greenhill Military Small Arms Data Book* (1999)
Calibre 9mm
Cartridge 9x19, rimless
Operation Recoil, semi-automatic only
Locking system Modified Browning tipping barrel
Length 7.72mm (196in)
Weight 875g (31.0oz) with empty magazine
Barrel 112mm (4.41in), 6 grooves, right-hand twist
Magazine 15-round detachable box
Muzzle velocity 350m/sec* (1148ft/sec*) with ball ammunition

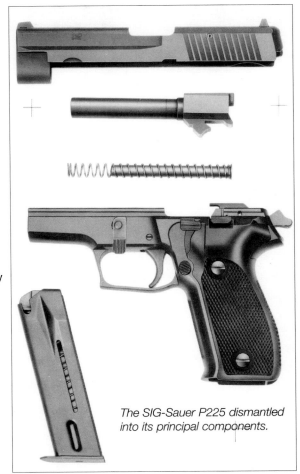

The SIG-Sauer P225 dismantled into its principal components.

The original Ruger pistol, the P85, developed to compete in the US JSSAP trials that eventually standardised the Beretta 92F, was perfected too late for inclusion. However, the new gun was accepted enthusiastically by the commercial market and has been made in a variety of guises.

The 9mm Ruger KP95D (stainless-steel, double action).

The action is a variation of the Browning tipping-barrel system, amalgamating a squared barrel-block (inspired, no doubt, by the SIG-Sauer pistol) with a link-type depressor. The safety catch and the magazine release are duplicated, though the slide-stop will be found only on the left side of the frame.

The first guns were made in New England, but production has now switched to a new purpose-built site in Arizona. Ruger has always prided itself on keeping abreast of manufacturing technology and the pistols embody a variety of precision investment castings. The frame of the P85 is steel, though the frame is an durable alloy; the P94 and P95, however, have synthetic one-piece grip/frame units. Introduced in 1996, the P95 can be supplied with a de-cocking lever, but the safety function is an integral part of the trigger mechanism, ensuring that the gun can be fired only in the final stages of a deliberate trigger pull. The 95 DAO is a modified version, designed solely for double-action firing.

Made by Sturm, Ruger & Co., Inc., Southport, Connecticut, and Prescott, Arizona, USA

Specification Semi-automatic pistol
Data from *Guns Digest,* 1997 edition
Calibre 9mm
Cartridge 9x19, rimless
Operation Recoil, semi-automatic only
Locking system Modified Browning tipping barrel
Length 185mm* (7.3in)
Weight 765g* (27.0oz) with empty magazine
Barrel 99mm* (3.9in), 6 grooves, right-hand twist
Magazine 10-round detachable box
Muzzle velocity 350m/sec* (1148ft/sec*) with ball ammunition

Semi-automatic pistols, modern style

This group contains the most innovative of modern handguns, embodying unusual features, particularly in the safety mechanism, and ground-breaking manufacturing techniques.

Dating from 1983, this is, perhaps, the greatest handgun success of its generation. Designed by an otherwise unknown Austrian, Gaston Glock, and made by an unfashionable engineering business, it has been made in a variety of forms and chamberings. The basic operating system is a straightforward adaptation of the Colt-Browning, with a simplified cam-finger depressor and a squared barrel-block lock inspired by the SIG-Sauers.

The most interesting feature is the abandonment of applied safety features – usually deemed mandatory to reduce the chance of accidents – in favour of a grip safety. This takes the form of a small supplementary blade set into the trigger lever, which, when the firer squeezes the trigger, allows the striker to be released; Glock pistols cannot fire if they are dropped, even on concrete, as the trigger mechanism is disabled. This system gives the Glock the same total safety/instant first-shot capability of a transfer-bar revolver.

The extensive use of synthetic material in the frame and slide is another innovative feature, though, contrary to rumours that swept the world when the pistols first appeared, the inclusion of a steel barrel and metal springs (not to mention the cartridges!) allows metal detectors to register the presence of a Glock satisfactorily.

Glock pistols have been made in several chamberings and a variety of sizes, including the Model 19, 174mm overall, and the Model 26 Sub-Compact, which is 160mm long and has a ten-round magazine contained in an abbreviated grip.

The Glock Sub-Compact pistols, .40 S&W Model 27 (top) and 9mm Parabellum Model 26 (bottom).

Made by Glock GmbH, Deutsch-Wagram, Austria
Specification Semi-automatic pistol
Data from Ian Hogg, *The Greenhill Military Small Arms Data Book* (1999)
Calibre 9mm
Cartridge 9x19, rimless
Operation Recoil, semi-automatic only
Locking system Modified Browning tipping barrel
Length 186mm (7.32in)
Weight 625g (22.0oz) with empty magazine
Barrel 114mm (4.50in), 6 grooves, right-hand twist
Magazine 17-round detachable box
Muzzle velocity 385m/sec (1263ft/sec) with ball ammunition

This interesting gun, announced in 1995, represents a considerable departure from standard handgun practice and its influence may only now be beginning to be felt. The Five-seveN® not only chambers a powerful cartridge, but it is also a delayed blowback.

Made of a steel slide and a composite frame/grip unit, the pistol accompanied the P90® personal-defence weapon, a leading contender for the amalgamated role of submachine gun and light automatic rifle. These hybrids are usually

lacking in features (cf., Swiss Stg 90/SIG 551), but the approach taken by FN challenges this.

Clearly, a change in military policy is necessary before the P90®, and by extension the Five-seveN®, can be accepted. The cartridge does not have the long-range performance of even the standardised 5.56x45 pattern and the personal-defence weapon is much more cumbersome than the Heckler & Koch MP5, the submachine gun favoured by most counter-terrorist units. However, commonality of ammunition is potentially a great bonus for logisticians. FN began the work, others are already experimenting similarly (e.g., Heckler & Koch) and only time will tell whether success will follow.

The pistol is striker-fired, relying on the trigger pull to compress the spring before the striker

can be released. This provides a safety feature reminiscent of the Austro-Hungarian Roth-Steyr cavalry pistol of 1907. A loaded-chamber indicator is also fitted as standard.

Made by FN Herstal SA, Herstal-lèz-
  Liège, Belgium
Specification Semi-automatic pistol
  Data from the manufacturer's website,
  accessed in July 2001
Calibre 5.7mm
Cartridge 5.7x28 P90®, rimless
Operation Delayed blowback
Locking system Cams delay the opening
  of the breech
Length 208mm (8.19in*)
Weight 618g (21.8oz*) with empty
  magazine, 744g (26.2oz*) with loaded
  magazine
Barrel 122.5mm (4.82in*), 6 grooves,
  right-hand twist
Magazine 20-round detachable box
Muzzle velocity 650m/sec (2133ft/sec)
  with ball ammunition

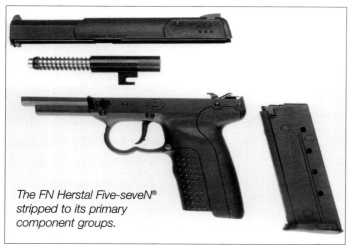

The FN Herstal Five-seveN® stripped to its primary component groups.

Perhaps developed before its time, this was a large striker-fired self-cocking blowback pistol, with a synthetic frame and an alloy slide. Its most distinctive feature, at least in its military guise (VP70M, *Militärausführung* – military pattern), was a holster stock incorporating a connector for the burst-firing capability built into the trigger mechanism of the pistol. However, this could only be activated when the stock was fitted and the radial selector on the upper arm of the stock, above the cut-out allowing the firer to grip the pistol, had been moved to '3'; set on '1', the weapon fired semi-automatically.

Also made in a semi-automatic 'civilian' guise (VP70Z, *Zivilausführung* – commercial pattern), which lacked the burst-firing feature, this Heckler & Koch design was abandoned after only a few thousand had been made.

Made by Heckler & Koch GmbH, Oberndorf/Neckar, Germany
Specification Semi-automatic pistol
Data from Ian Hogg, *The Greenhill Military Small Arms Data Book* (1999)
Calibre 9mm
Cartridge 9x19, rimless
Operation Blowback

Locking system None
Length 204mm (8.03in)
Weight 800g (28.0oz) with empty magazine
Barrel 105mm (4.13in), 4 grooves, right-hand twist
Magazine 8-round detachable box
Rate of fire Bursts only
Muzzle velocity 350m/sec (1148ft/sec) with ball ammunition

The Heckler & Koch VP70M, with its shoulder stock/holster attached. Note the radial selector on the front upper tip of the stock.

Heckler & Koch USP

Announced in 1994, this is the first Heckler & Koch pistol to incorporate a breech lock, previous designs being simple or hesitation blowbacks. A finger beneath the fashionably squared barrel-block, which rises into the slide aperture, acts in concert with a cam surface to break the lock simply by pulling the block downward. This allows the slide to reciprocate alone, returning to strip a new round from the magazine into the chamber.

The USP embodies a patented recoil-damping system, consisting of concentric buffer springs beneath the barrel, and has a hammer in the firing system instead of a striker. The controls are ambidextrous, the frame is a durable polymer and the slide is a steel investment casting.

Chambered for the 9x19 (9mm Parabellum), .40 S&W or .45 ACP cartridges, the USP is available in several guises – owing to its modular construction, which acts like a kit of selectable parts. Optional features include the de-cocking system and the manual safety catch, which may be on either side of the frame or ambidextrous. Lockwork may be single action, double action (exposed hammer), or self-cocking (hammerless) only.

The underside of the fore-end is grooved to accept a laser designator or similar accessories, and the sights can be adjusted by sliding them laterally in their

The Heckler & Koch USP in its long-barrelled US SOCOM Mark 23 Model 0 form, complete with silencer.

dovetails. Heckler & Koch delivered 7500 modified .45-calibre USP to the US Special Operations Command (SOCOM) in 1997, fitted with combination laser designators/light projectors and silencers. Known on the US inventory as the 'Offensive Handgun Weapons System' (OHWS) or 'Pistols, Mark 23 Model 0' in naval parlance, they are still serving the special forces.

Derivatives of the USP, the P8 and the compact P10 (9x19), have been adopted by the German police to replace the P5 (Walther), P6 (SIG-Sauer P226) and P7 (Heckler & Koch P7M8).

Made by Heckler & Koch GmbH, Oberndorf/Neckar, Germany

Specification Semi-automatic pistol

Data from the manufacturer's website, accessed in July 2001

Calibre 9mm

Cartridge 9x19, rimless

Operation Recoil, semi-automatic only

Locking system Modified Browning tipping barrel

Length 194mm (7.64in*)

Weight 720g (25.4oz*) without magazine

Barrel 108mm (4.25in*), 4 grooves, right-hand twist

Magazine 15-round detachable box

Muzzle velocity 350m/sec (1148ft/sec*) with ball ammunition

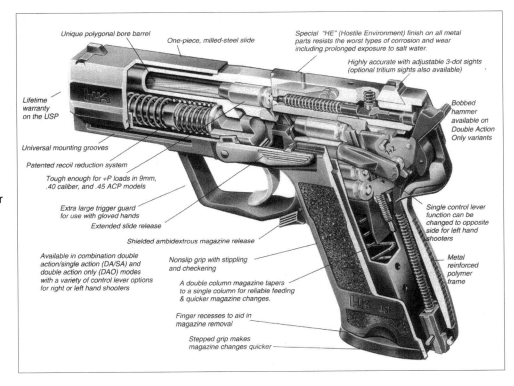

Unique polygonal bore barrel

One-piece, milled-steel slide

Special "HE" (Hostile Environment) finish on all metal parts resists the worst types of corrosion and wear including prolonged exposure to salt water

Highly accurate with adjustable 3-dot sights (optional tritium sights also available)

Lifetime warranty on the USP

Bobbed hammer available on Double Action Only variants

Universal mounting grooves

Patented recoil reduction system

Tough enough for +P loads in 9mm, .40 caliber, and .45 ACP models

Extra large trigger guard for use with gloved hands

Extended slide release

Shielded ambidextrous magazine release

Single control lever function can be changed to opposite side for left hand shooters

Metal reinforced polymer frame

Available in combination double action/single action (DA/SA) and double action only (DAO) modes with a variety of control lever options for right or left hand shooters

Nonslip grip with stippling and checkering

A double column magazine tapers to a single column for reliable feeding & quicker magazine changes.

Finger recesses to aid in magazine removal

Stepped grip makes magazine changes quicker

An exploded view of the Heckler & Koch USP, from the H&K magazine published in the USA.

SHOTGUNS

The shotgun has a lengthy pedigree going back to the earliest days of the muzzleloader, when bird-shot – often simply shards of metal – could be used to provide food. Regularisation came first with the advent of mass-produced shot, which could be made in graded sizes for differing purposes, and then with the introduction of breech-loading Lefaucheux-type pinfire shotguns. These began a line that can be traced directly to the double-barrelled guns of today, even though the original side-by-side barrel layout has been challenged by the superposed or over/under type.

The use of shotguns for military and police purposes has also been established for many years. One of the first uses, making best use of the ability of small shot to spread as it left the muzzle, was to guard convicts (replacing the blunderbuss) or arm sentries, in cases where standard ball cartridges would either have been too dangerous or, particularly where single-shot weapons were concerned, too liable to miss a target that might be half seen in darkness. Cartridges were regularly loaded for these purposes; e.g., buckshot ammunition for the Snider, the Martini-Henry or the Lee-Enfield.

The use of the shotgun as an offensive weapon, though Wild West notables such as John H. 'Doc' Holliday favoured it, was due largely to the First World War. It was also due to the emergence of efficient magazine-feed shotguns of a type unknown in Europe, where the traditional sporting gun remained pre-eminent. The first successful magazine-feed shotguns were lever action, designed by John Browning, and made by the Winchester Repeating Arms Company. However, these represented a developmental dead end; much more successful in the long term was the pump- or slide-action pattern, credited to Sylvester Roper and Christopher Spencer (though a court case bitterly contested with Andrew Burgess revealed earlier patents).

Slide-action guns had tubular magazines in the butt (rare) or beneath the barrel (common) and could fire up to eight rounds as fast as the action could be operated. This was enough to interest the military and the US Army tested a rifle version of the Roper-Spencer design in the early 1890s. In addition, it elevated the humble shotgun to the status of effectual offensive weapon. The mechanically operated repeater was followed in the first decade of the twentieth century by the first semi-automatics, among them the Browning design exploited by FN and Remington.

Slide-action and semi-automatic guns had become comparatively common in the USA when the First World War began and it was a short step to militarising them by the addition of bayonets. The Remington Model was particularly popular, accepting bayonets ranging from the Russian 1891-pattern socket to the 1917-pattern US Army sword. All were chambered for the same 12-bore ammunition, but one of the merits of the shotgun – indeed, still its greatest asset – lay in the ability to fire projectiles ranging from the smallest dust shot to an awesome slug. The smooth-bored barrel limits accuracy to short distances, but also allows buckshot to spread sufficiently to reduce the effects of aiming errors.

Shotguns were purchased in huge numbers in the First World War and, though customarily relegated to guard or behind-the-lines usage, were occasionally tried in the trenches. Short, handy and deadly at close range, they were often more suited to the cramped conditions than a cumbersome infantry rifle. Others, often cut down behind the pistol grip, were used in the early days of air warfare to pepper the fragile aeroplanes of the day.

After the fighting had ended, the shotgun was returned to sporting world – through the shortened sawn-off form rapidly entered the armoury of the underworld. Little was done until the Second World War began and, even then, the story was much the same as it had been more than 20 years earlier: second-line duties. Combat roles were not envisaged for the shotgun, partly because of the demise of trench fighting and partly owing to the widespread issue of light semi-automatic rifles and submachine guns. This was particularly true in the USA, the principal manufacturing centre of magazine shotguns, where the issue of more than 6 million M1 Carbines made widespread issue of shotguns unnecessary. But there were theatres where the same combination of handiness and close-range firepower was attractive (clearing the Japanese-held islands in the Pacific, for example).

The same has been true of wars such as Korea and Vietnam. However, the rise of the combat shotgun owes most to the development of special forces and the SWAT squads. The virtues of the magazine shotgun remain just as they were in 1918: close-range firepower, an ability to handle a far wider range of ammunition than a traditional infantry rifle and the spreading quality that minimises aiming errors. In addition, a particular consideration in urban environments, the buckshot-loaded shotgun has a comparatively short range and does not present the same likelihood of accidental kills at long range as other weapons; the bullet from even a 5.56mm-calibre infantry rifle is capable of travelling 2 miles.

Trends in combat shotgun design have fluctuated. For many years, only the slide-action pattern (with an occasional semi-automatic) was favoured, largely owing to the ability to eject a misfired cartridge and reload manually. A misfire in a semi-automatic is rarely as easy to clear. A problem has also arisen from the design of modern shotgun ammunition. Most modern patterns have bodies made of plastic, only the base being metal, usually an alloy of brass. Though rigid enough for normal purposes, plastic-bodied ammunition is prone to deform in a nose-to-tail tube magazine either under the influence of recoil or jolting, if, for example, the butt of the shotgun is struck accidentally on the ground or within a confined space.

Though bolt-action shotguns are made in small numbers and have even been issued for police use, they have never been popular. This is mainly due to the slow acceptance of the bolt system in the USA, which only really took hold in the sporting-gun market after the US troops had been demobilised after the end of the First World War. It cannot be denied that the slide mechanism is faster than the bolt; however, bolt-action guns are traditionally fed from box magazines. A well-designed box magazine feeds better than a tube and is much easier to replenish. Though it protrudes from the

The Franchi PA-3 general-purpose/combat shotgun has been made in a variety of guises, including this long-barrelled example.

stock – particularly as 12-bore shotgun cases have a large diameter – the cartridges are not prone to crushing. In addition, if a cut-off is fitted, single special-purpose cartridges can be inserted in the chamber when required. This is an attractive feature compared with a multi-round tube magazine, which cannot be so easily emptied.

However, the bolt-action shotgun is still awkward to use. Solutions have included slide-action guns with box magazines and an increasing interest in semi-automatic guns. The need for combatworthy weapons has also led designers away from traditions towards assault rifles. One of the best known of all combat shotguns, the Franchi SPAS 12 (Special Purpose Assault Shotgun) can be found with folding stocks, ventilated handguards and a variety of muzzle fittings. It retains a tube magazine, but a later design, the SPAS 15, relies on a box. The same trends can be seen with Beretta and similar designs.

Some of the more unusual combat/personal-defence designs have featured revolving or rotary magazines, often in the form of a cylinder. These usually bring a penalty in the form of weight, but the separation of the vulnerable plastic-bodied cartridges in individual chambers does have advantages. Attempts have also been made to shorten shotguns – which

can be unwieldy – by adopting a bullpup layout, with the pistol grip ahead of the magazine, and to improve the sights. Sight lines have been raised, often by incorporating a sight channel with a carrying handle, and brackets for optical or intensifier sights have been added. Equally popular, and well suited to essentially short-range weapons, has been the addition of snap-shooting sights, including red-dot collimators or laser designators, to the receiver.

Development of the shotgun continues, with the incorporation of synthetic components and the development of ammunition. Several attempts have been made to reintroduce all-metal cartridges – a reversion to nineteenth century practice! – and even to develop rimless cases that would improve feed from box magazines. Each change that is made, however, moves the design of the shotgun, and its ability to fire virtually any commercially available 12-bore cartridge, another step away from ubiquity.

The gun must be strong and durable enough to withstand active service. The slide-action guns used during the First World War were adequate and the modern combat shotgun retains many of their virtues. A variety of corrosion-resisting finishes have been developed in recent years, in particular, the widespread

introduction of stainless steel. The advent of synthetic components, though not without some mistakes, has simplified the construction of stocks and butts and some designs now have all-enveloping frames/stocks of sturdy polymers. This is an area in which progress is sure to be made in the next decade.

The gun must contain as few parts as possible. The pursuit of simplicity is generally desirable, but the uncertainty of the combat role of a shotgun and the tendency to add features to existing designs has sometimes tended to complicate what is essentially an ultra-simple weapon. This is particularly true of shotguns that are selectably slide-action/semi-automatic and is sometimes also true of those that employ folding butts. Against this, the development of synthetic butt/frame units, relying on sturdy injection-mouldings, should enable non-essential parts to be reduced to a minimum.

The gun must be easy to make and economical in terms of materials. Modern shotguns are usually designed with ease of production in mind and may embody investment castings and injection-moulded synthetic furniture. Though the first cost of tooling may be high, the unit cost over lengthy production runs is usually reduced compared with more traditional steel-and-wood construction. And, in addition, the strength of the critical components is sometimes increased.

The gun must be simple to operate and thus easily managed. Modern guns are customarily as simple as their predecessors, except in cases where sophisticated optical or intensifier sights are fitted and where muzzle fixtures – grenade launchers, for example – are used.

The gun must be as compact as possible. Shotguns are rarely ultra-compact, especially the tube-magazine patterns in which a desirable reduction in barrel length is accompanied by a commensurate, but undesirable reduction in magazine capacity. The size of the 12-bore cartridge also makes box magazines very bulky, particularly when allied with attempts to increase magazine capacity to ten rounds or more. The most usual concessions to reductions in length are folding butts or pistol-grip butt substitutes.

The gun must handle well. The conventional slide-action shotgun shoulders surprisingly well, usually weighing empty only about 7lb. However, actuating the slide often displaces aim – one of the few areas where bolt-action designs may have advantages – there is a perceptible change in the balance point as the cartridges are expended and the trend has been towards large-capacity detachable box magazines. These do not have a beneficial effect on handling, as they protrude beneath the receiver.

The gun must not jam in operation. Modern shotguns are surprisingly reliable, though slide-action and semi-automatic guns can be vulnerable to the crushing of plastic-bodied cartridges in a way that traditional two-barrel guns and the revolver-type autoloaders are not. The introduction of metal-case cartridges would reduce the problems, but only at the expense of ammunition availability.

The gun must be easy to clean and simple to maintain. Most modern guns are easy to field-strip and maintain, though there is a trend towards additional complexity and, therefore, an increase in potential trouble spots.

The gun must be accurate, sufficiently powerful and offer sufficient range. Another of the areas in which compromises must be made, this must take into account that shotguns are essentially ultra short-range weapons. The potential power of the 12-bore cartridge, which is much larger than a conventional 5.56x45 rifle round, all too often persuades military authorities – in recent years, keen to develop all-purpose infantry weapons – to try to extend the capabilities of a shotgun well beyond its traditional limits. The shotgun cannot replace either the infantry rifle or the grenade launcher and is certainly much less versatile than the combination of the two!

The gun must carry as much ammunition as possible. The shotgun suffers from the weight restrictions imposed by its cartridge and, in most traditional designs, by the length of the under-barrel tube magazine. The development of detachable magazines theoretically resolves this problem, but only at the expense of a large projecting box. Realistically, cartridge capacities are restricted to a maximum of seven or eight in a tube or ten to twelve in a box.

Details of only a few typical shotguns are given here. Additional information can be found in another Greenhill Military Manual – Leroy Thompson, *Combat Shotguns* (2002).

Traditional slide-action shotguns

These customarily have commercial antecedents, though concessions are made to corrosion resistance. Sights are usually simple, slide handles are plain and finish is often non-reflective.

Beretta RS202

The Beretta is a conventional slide-action shotgun with a tube magazine. It has been made in several sporting guises, but has also been offered for personal defence or police use. In this form it has a plain wood butt and a ribbed cylindrical slide handle. The safety catch will be found in the front web of the trigger guard, with a separate breech-block latch protruding on the left and a cartridge-latch button on the right side of the receiver beneath the ejection port.

Steel components have a black Bruniton finish, alloy parts being anodised. Sling swivels are customarily found under the pistol-grip butt and on the tip of the magazine tube. Sights consist of a groove in the receiver-top and a small blade (police pattern) at the muzzle, though guns have been made with Williams peep sights on the receiver.

Made by Fabbrica d'Armi Pietro Beretta SpA, Gardone V.T. (Brescia), Italy
Specification Slide-action shotgun
Data from manufacturer's leaflet
RS202, RS202P. Istruzione per l'uso… (dated January 1984)
Calibre .753 (12-bore)
Cartridge 12x70, rimmed
Operation Manual, single shot only
Locking system Displacement of breech block
Length 1020mm (40.16in*)
Weight 3.245kg* (7.15lb*) with empty magazine
Barrel 520mm (20.47in*), smooth-bored
Magazine 6-round tube beneath barrel
Muzzle velocity NA

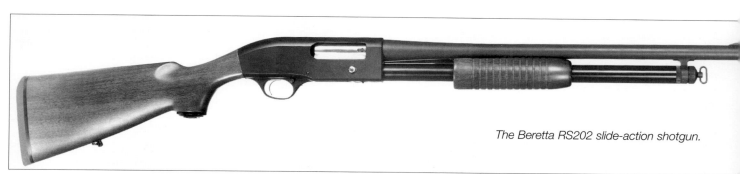

The Beretta RS202 slide-action shotgun.

The Mossberg Model 500 Persuader™, with matt finish and a full-length magazine tube.

Mossberg, after making large numbers of rimfire and centrefire rifles, now concentrates solely on shotguns, ranging from high-quality sporting guns to military/police weapons. The standard guns have twin extractors, duplicated cartridge latches and a sliding safety catch on the upper rear of the receiver.

The Model 500 Persuader™ or Police Persuader has a full-length magazine tube, simple hardwood furniture, a ventilated butt pad and a sliding safety catch on top of the receiver. One good feature is the mounting of the front sling swivel on a magazine-support band attached to the underside of the barrel, which is better than the customary end-cap mount that can strain the magazine. The second swivel on the Mossberg lies conventionally beneath the butt. The sights on this particular model are basic, but others in the range will be found with Williams ramp-type peep sights on the receiver.

Mossberg also makes a 'Cruiser' variant, with a pistol grip substituted for the butt, as well as Mariner™ and Intimidator™ patterns, the former with a Teflon/nickel Marinecote™ finish and the latter with a red-dot laser projector built into the fore-end. Mossberg shotguns outperformed all others in US military endurance trials (MILSPEC 3443E) and are regularly purchased for special duties.

Made by O.F. Mossberg & Sons, Inc., North Haven, Connecticut, USA
Specification Slide-action shotgun
Data from the manufacturer's catalogue, *1992 Shooting Systems*
Calibre .753 (12-bore)
Cartridge 12x70, rimmed
Operation Manual, single shot only
Locking system Displacement of breech block
Length 978mm* (38.5in)
Weight 3.06kg* (6.75lb) with empty magazine
Barrel 470mm* (18.5in), smooth-bore
Magazine 6-round tube beneath barrel
Muzzle velocity NA

Winchester M1300 Marine Defender™ USA

Another of the many US-made slide-action designs, this offers a blend of traditional design and ultra-modern corrosion-resistant materials: stainless steel for the barrel and magazine tube, matted steel for the receiver and polymers for the ribbed slide handle and pistol grip butt. Unlike many slide-action guns, which are locked by displacing a breech block into the top inner surface of the slide, the Winchester has a front-locking rotating bolt with two diametrically opposed lugs. The action bars are doubled to give a smooth operating stroke.

Advertised as a 'Pump Action Security Shotgun', the M1300 has proved popular. But it would undoubtedly benefit from a less gaudy appearance, which has no place in a SWAT/special forces

The Winchester M1300 Stainless Marine Defender™, 'Pump Action Security Shotgun'.

environment! The current tendency is towards matt-finish metalwork and non-reflective synthetic furniture and even towards camouflage finish for specific-theatre use.

Made by US Repeating Arms Company, Morgan, Utah, USA
Specification Slide-action shotgun
Data from Ian Hogg, *The Greenhill Military Small Arms Data Book* (1999)

Calibre .753
Cartridge 12-bore, rimless
Operation Manual, single shot only
Locking system Rotating bolt
Length 981mm* (38.63in)
Weight 3.06kg* (6.75lb) with empty magazine
Barrel 457mm* (18.0in), smooth-bored
Magazine 8-round tube beneath barrel
Muzzle velocity NA

Traditional bolt-action shotguns

This is one of the few modern representatives of the bolt-action genre, which has a pedigree dating back to the nineteenth century. Its advantages include good primary extraction, owing to the camming action of the bolt as it opens,

and the ability to work the action while prone with the minimum of fuss. Disadvantages include the awkwardness of the bolt motion compared with the simple push-pull of a slide-action rival.

The Savage Model 210FT bolt-action shotgun, typifying an uncommon genre that has specific uses.

This is an interesting 1996-vintage derivative of the well-established Savage Model 110 bolt-action cartridge rifle, designed by Nicholas Brewer in the 1950s. This design has a safety catch on the tang and a cocking indicator protruding from the right side of the receiver bridge.

Intended more for sporting use, shotguns of this type would suit police teams armed, for example, with Savage sniping rifles. It also demonstrates the currently fashionable application of camouflage finish (this is a RealTree™ pattern) on a fibreglass resin stock, with swivel eyes in the customary positions beneath the butt and the fore-end.

The large-diameter slab-like magazine and rudimentary sights mark this as a shotgun instead of the similar looking cartridge rifles, but the barrel has slow-pitch rifling (one turn in 35in) and rails for optical sight mounts are provided to improve accuracy when firing slugs.

Made by the Savage Arms Company, Inc., Westfield, Massachusetts, USA
Specification Bolt-action shotgun
Data from *Guns Digest* (1997 edition)
Calibre .753 (12-bore)
Cartridge 12x76, rimmed
Operation Manual, single shot only
Locking system Lugs on a rotating bolt
Length 1105mm* (43.5in)
Weight 3.4kg* (7.50lb) with empty magazine
Barrel 610mm* (24.0in), 6 grooves, right-hand twist
Magazine 3-round detachable box
Muzzle velocity NA

Traditional semi-automatic shotguns

Benelli M-1 Super 90 {#benelli-m-1-super-90}

Italy

This is a typical modern semi-automatic design, made by one of the world's most experienced manufacturers. Derived from a sporting gun, which shows in its overall lines, the Benelli is also made as a slide-action M-3 Super 90. The M-1 operates in an interesting way, relying on an inertia block within the breech to move *forward* during the initial stages of recoil before the being forced back to open the breech and rotate the locking lugs out of engagement with the receiver.

A typical example has synthetic furniture, with a sling anchor on the butt side and a matted metalwork. The sights consist of a simple open notch and a blade on top of the muzzle, though the M-1 Super 90 Combat has a pistol-grip butt and a Williams receiver-sight protected by prominent wings. In this particular case, the front sight is raised on a short rib and tritium night-sight inserts are optional. A cross-bolt safety lies in the rear web of the trigger guard, the tip of the cartridge-drop lever, above the front web of the

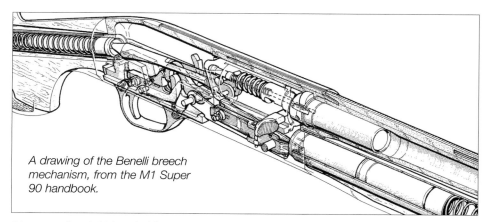

A drawing of the Benelli breech mechanism, from the M1 Super 90 handbook.

trigger on the right hand side, acts as a cocking indicator, and a carrier-lock protrudes from the receiver beneath the cocking handle.

Made by Benelli Armi SpA, Urbino, Italy
Specification Semi-automatic shotgun
  Data from *Gun Digest* (1997 edition)
Calibre .753 (12-bore)
Cartridge 12x70, rimmed

Operation Delayed blowback, single shot only
Locking system Rotating bolt
Length 1010mm* (39.75in)
Weight 3.175kg* (7.0lb) with empty magazine
Barrel 470mm* (18.50in), smooth-bored
Magazine 5-round tube beneath barrel
Muzzle velocity NA

Modern designs of shotgun

Beretta M3P   Italy

The Beretta M3P dual-action (manual/auto-loading) shotgun, built on a Benelli action.

This is a step forward from the RS202 M2, offering the firer the option of gas-operated auto-loading or manual slide operation on the basis of a Benelli action. The magazine is a detachable box. A safety catch lies through the rear web of the trigger guard, a cocking indicator protrudes beneath the right side of the receiver above the front web and a release catch protrudes from a housing behind the magazine. The function/mode selector is a radial lever immediately ahead of the fore-end. The sights are simple, while the fore-end/slider, pistol grip and upward-folding butt are all sturdy synthetic components.

Made by Fabbrica d'Armi Pietro Beretta SpA, Gardone V.T. (Brescia), Italy

Specification Autoloading or slide-action shotgun
Data from an undated draft of a manufacturer's leaflet, c. 1990
Calibre .753 (12-bore)
Cartridge 12x70, rimmed

Operation Delayed blowback or manual, single shot only
Locking system Rotating bolt
Length 940mm (37.01in*) butt extended; 685mm (26.97in*) butt folded
Weight 3.540kg (7.80lb*) empty
Barrel 400mm (15.75in*), smooth-bored
Magazine 5-round detachable box
Muzzle velocity NA

The Beretta RS202 M2 slide-action combat shotgun.

This is an attempt to update what is otherwise a surprisingly traditional gun. Its essence is a conventional slide-action mechanism, with a transverse safety catch through the trigger-guard web and a cartridge-latch button on the side of the receiver under the front of the ejection port. The pistol grip undoubtedly improves control and the side-folding metal-tube butt shortens overall length. A ventilated sheet-steel handguard protects the barrel, simultaneously doubling as a mount for the simple sights. This particular gun also has a flash-hider on the muzzle. The pistol grip and the ribbed slide handle are synthetic.

Made by Fabbrica d'Armi Pietro Beretta SpA, Gardone V.T. (Brescia), Italy

Specification Slide-action shotgun Data from an undated draft of a manufacturer's leaflet, *c.* 1990

Calibre .753 (12-bore)

Cartridge 12x70, rimmed

Operation Manual, single shot only

Locking system Displacement of the breech block

Length 1050mm (41.34in*)

Weight 3.850kg (8.49lb*) with empty magazine

Barrel 615mm (24.21in*) including flash-hider, smooth-bored

Magazine 6-round tube beneath barrel

Muzzle velocity NA

This answers requests for an ultra-compact personal-defence/assault weapon amalgamating the advantages of a shotgun with the portability of a submachine gun. The folding metal stock/pistol grip and the short barrel keep dimensions to a minimum, though at the expense of magazine capacity. The length of the magazine tube prevents a conventional ribbed cylindrical slide-handle being used, so its function has been combined with an additional pistol grip made of glass-filled resin. The principal safety catch is a large radial lever on the front right side of the elongated trigger-guard web, though a 'quick release' safety protrudes into the trigger guard.

This gun has a sling swivel on the magazine end cap and an adjustable choke on the muzzle. However, the PA-3 has been made in several versions, the PA-3/345 and PA-3/470 (the three-figure numbers refer to barrel length in millimetres) having conventional ribbed-cylinder slide handles. Finish is customarily sandblasted and phosphated to give the metal parts a non-reflecting surface.

Made by Luigi Franchi SpA, Divisione Sistemi Difensivi, Fornaci (Brescia), Italy
Specification Slide-action shotgun
Data from a manufacturer's leaflet (*c.* 1985)
Calibre .753 (12-bore)
Cartridge 12x70, rimmed
Operation Manual, single shot only
Locking system Displacement of a locking-block in the bolt
Length 465mm (18.31in*)
Weight 2.950kg (6.50lb*) with empty magazine
Barrel 215mm (8.46in*), smooth-bored
Magazine 3-round tube beneath barrel
Muzzle velocity NA

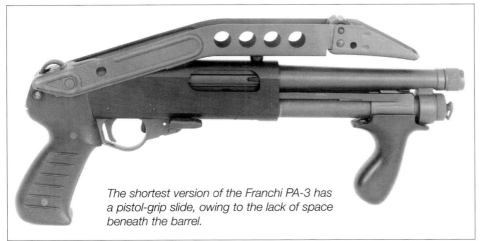

The shortest version of the Franchi PA-3 has a pistol-grip slide, owing to the lack of space beneath the barrel.

Franchi SPAS-12 Italy

The Franchi SPAS-12 combat shotgun, a selectable manual/auto-loading design. The patented hook on the butt supports the arm during one-hand firing.

Made by Luigi Franchi SpA, Divisione
 Sistemi Difensivi, Fornaci (Brescia), Italy
Specification Autoloading/slide-action
 shotgun
 Data from a manufacturer's leaflet,
 SPAS 12 cal. 12x70 (12x2¾) (c. 1985)
Calibre .753 (12-bore)
Cartridge 12x70, rimmed
Operation Gas or manual, single shot
 only
Locking system Displacement of a
 locking block in the bolt
Length 930mm (36.61in*) butt extended;
 710mm (27.95in*) butt folded
Weight 4.150kg (9.15lb*) empty
Barrel 457mm* (18.00in), smooth-bored
Magazine 6-round tube beneath barrel
Muzzle velocity NA

Developed to satisfy the requirements of the US Naval Weapons Center Close Assault Weapon (CAW) and the Joint Service Small Arms Program (JSSAP) Rhino projects, this is now one of the best-known of all combat shotguns. Introduced in 1979, the SPAS-12 is a conventional design clothed in unconventional furniture. The folding butt has a distinctive configuration, with a special shoulder piece to facilitate one-handed operation by hooking under the firer's arm. The arms of the butt have four circular apertures each

side. The pistol grip and the slide handle are injection-moulded plastic, ergonomically shaped, while the ventilated handguard envelops the barrel and the magazine.

The dual manual safeties of the PA-3 are retained and a cartridge-latch button lies on the front right side of the receiver. The operating-mode selector button lies under the fore-end.

The gun illustrated has an adjustable choke at the muzzle and the customary rudimentary sights, but a variety of accessories can be obtained.

Franchi SPAS-15 Italy

The Franchi SPAS-15, an improved form of the SPAS-12, has a detachable box magazine instead of an under-barrel tube.

Made by Franchi Divisione Sistemi Difensivi, Fornaci (Brescia), Italy

Specification Autoloading/slide-action shotgun

Data from a manufacturer's leaflet, *SPAS 15 cal. 12x70 (12x2¾)* (dated December 1987)

Calibre .753 (12-bore)

Cartridge 12x70, rimmed

Operation Gas or manual, single shot only

Locking system Displacement of a locking block in the bolt

Length 915mm (36.02in*) butt extended; 700mm (27.56in*) butt folded

Weight 3.90kg (8.60lb*) with empty magazine

Barrel 406mm (16.0in), smooth-bored

Magazine 6-round detachable box

Muzzle velocity NA

Developed in 1984, incorporating lessons learned from the SPAS-12, this dual-action shotgun is a truly militarised shotgun. Superficially resembling the ArmaLite AR-15/M16 series, with straight-line configuration and the ramp of the open backsight doubling as a carrying handle, the SPAS-15 has a box magazine. The tubular butt folds sideways along the left side of the receiver, the cocking handle lies in a slot beneath the carrying handle and an automatic grip safety is set into the face of the pistol grip. Pressings and stampings reduce costs wherever possible, but the design has yet to gain the acceptance that greeted the SPAS-12 (q.v.). The SPAS-16 was similar, but restricted to semi-automatic operation. It was made only in small numbers.

INFANTRY RIFLES

Virtually all front-line armies are now equipped with 5.56mm assault rifles and, though some armies began the move away from 7.62x51 NATO in the 1980s, the change has only very recently occurred in Belgium, Germany and Italy. In the Germans' case, however, the tardy replacement of the 7.62mm G3 with the 5.56mm G36 was largely due to the protracted testing and sudden abandonment of the Heckler & Koch G11 caseless-cartridge rifle.

The gun must be strong and durable enough to withstand active service. Few problems have been reported with any of the current front-line rifle designs, except the very public condemnation of the manufacturing standards of the British L85A1 which has not, as yet, been openly supported by the army authorities. However, the French FA-MAS has also been the butt of criticism, owing to the perceived marginal security of its breech-closing mechanism and there has been occasional castigation of other weapons in the press. The value of an individual design is customarily implicit in its export successes, an area where the FAL, the M16 series — perhaps owing at least a little to

American pressure — the Steyr AUG and the Belgian FN FNC have been particularly successful. The Kalashnikov has been made in huge quantities and is generally regarded as an effectual design, but one wonders whether its success would have been as great had satellite and Soviet-bloc armies been allowed a choice!

The gun must contain as few parts as possible. Most modern rifles are comparatively simple, though the development of ambidextrous controls and, particularly, the incorporation of burst-firing capabilities in the trigger mechanism have balanced the introduction of simplified gas systems. However, experiments aimed at providing an ultra-rapid burst may yet prove that there is a limit to the complication desirable in a mass-issue weapon. The advent of grenade launchers such as the US M203 or the Heckler & Koch M79 has also added to complexity, but many are still of the clip-on type.

The gun must be easy to make and economical in terms of materials. The manufacture of rifles reflects much of what was said previously about pistols. Once again, quantity and the

technological sophistication of the manufacturing nation are the arbiters. The Kalashnikov rifles have traditionally departed the least from the 1950s yardstick, whereas production of the ArmaLite AR-15/M16 series required much more sophistication. Though guns such as the FN FNC, the Beretta AR70/90 and the SIG SG 550 series still cling largely to 'metal technology', the Austrian AUG and the new German G36 make far greater concessions to the use of synthetic materials.

The gun must be simple to operate and thus easily managed. Despite the introduction of burst-firing, grenade launching and other additional features, the modern rifle is essentially easy to use. The incorporation of integral optical sights (e.g., on the L85A1, AUG, G36) is generally reckoned to improve marksmanship, even though the magnification — only 1.5x in the case of the AUG — may be small. Burst firing is undeniably an additional complexity, but is, to some observers, more useful than fully automatic fire in a weapon that may weight less than 8lb.

The gun must be as compact as possible. This remains a vexed question. The bullpup configuration,

These Royal Marines, pictured in the Falklands Islands in 1982, carry L1A1 rifles and bulky SS20 electro-optical sights.

with the chamber all but alongside the firer's cheek and the magazine behind the trigger group, has not found universal popularity. It prevents the gun being fired from the left shoulder unless the direction of ejection has been changed and raises safety concerns in the event of a cartridge failure that are still largely unanswered. Embedding the mechanism in a synthetic stock (e.g., AUG) dampens vibration effectively enough, but only purchasers of the AUG, the FA-MAS and the British L85A1 seem to agree that the reduction in overall length redeem the drawbacks of the bullpup design.

The gun must handle well. Handling qualities are subjective. The bullpups handle oddly, as the centre of gravity lies farther back than expected. The AUG, which is comparatively light, and the extra-short FA-MAS are better in this respect than the L85A1. There is little to choose between the conventional designs, though the long slender but relatively light M16A1 is generally reckoned better than most. The first-generation self-loading rifles such as the 7.62mm FAL and G3 were heavier than the 5.56mm group and, in the case of the G3, the excessive depth from the top of the receiver to the trigger could give an unbalancing effect. Ergonomics are important to a rifle designer and it will be interesting to see what the next generation of small arms brings; the slab-sided Heckler & Koch G11, praiseworthy though it may have been technically, was an awkward gun to handle.

The gun must not jam in operation. Modern rifles are relatively jam-free, but this depends on the quality of the ammunition. Historical problems with the M16 are well known, but are now resolved. However, the high chamber pressures generated by the 5.56x45 cartridge have caused extraction problems in many rifles, including the FN CAL and the SIG SG 530, both regarded as failures, and the FA-MAS and G33/G41 series, cured in the latter group by fluting the chambers.

The gun must be easy to clean and simple to maintain. Most rifles are easily field-stripped, particularly those, such as the SIG patterns, that hinge open at the touch of a button. A move away from direct-impingement gas operation has been made by almost everyone except the manufacturers of the ArmaLites, seeking to minimise fouling, but this is a compromise; the best solution, which has the merit of simplicity, is the most direct passage from the bore to the breech block and a rigorous maintenance regime. Propellant fouling is just one of the problems faced under field conditions, where the effects of snow, ice, mud, water or sand may be far worse.

The gun must be accurate, sufficiently powerful and offer sufficient range. Arguments have raged for years about the optimum combination of accuracy, range, recoil and cartridge weight. Wedded for a long time to the 7.62x51 NATO rounds, many armies have settled on the 5.56x45 pattern. However, attempts are still occasionally made to find a better solution to the complicated problems that face weapons designers and research is currently underway into 'second optimum' solutions that can be chambered in all-purpose weapons intended to replace the infantry rifle, the submachine gun and the handgun; the FN 5.7x28 and the Heckler & Koch/Dynamit Nobel 4.6x30 patterns are typical of these. However, neither offers much in the way of long-range accuracy; and there is a trend towards specialist rounds such as .300 Winchester Magnum or .338 Lapua Magnum for sniping rifles!

This problem is by no means new and is, perhaps, insuperable. There is no ideal solution that would range from a handgun to a light support weapon: there are still many who would point to cartridges such as the abortive British 6.25mm of the 1960s as the best guess.

The gun must carry as much ammunition as possible. The weight of ammunition that an individual soldier can be expected to carry in battlefield conditions is a limiting arbiter of this problem, together with the weight of the gun/loaded magazine combination, ideally no more than 4.5kg (10lb). Twenty-round magazines were the practicable maximum in the days of the 7.62x51 cartridges, whereas 30 rounds is more common with 5.56x45. The Soviets, the Russians and their allies have experimented with 40-round magazines for Kalashnikov rifles and light machine-guns and a few 50- or even 100-round drum magazines have been tried. Some would say that groups of 20-round magazines that fix together laterally are a better answer, as their protrusion beneath the gun is substantially less that the 30-round type, and the ability of an individual soldier to carry loads can be handled simply by clipping magazines together.

Details of only a few typical rifles are given here. Additional information can be found in another Greenhill Military Manual – John Walter, *Modern Military Rifles* (2001).

Steyr AUG   Austria

The Steyr AUG with an Oldelft electro-optical sight above the receiver.

A futuristic design that still looks ultra-modern, decades after its introduction, the AUG has been successful in Austria and Australia, where it is made under licence. The rifle is a bullpup, with the magazine behind the pistol grip, beneath the firer's cheek, and a fixed-power optical sight carried high above the receiver. The receiver is an aluminium casting, with steel inserts to support the barrel lugs and bolt guides, set in a synthetic butt/grip unit. A supplementary grip attached to the barrel can be folded down ahead of the trigger guard, which is formed integrally with the grip/frame and envelops the entire hand. The safety catch runs laterally above the pistol grip and fire selection is a function of the trigger: a half-pressure gives single shots, pulling the trigger back to its limit allows the gun to fire automatically. A transparent plastic magazine allows the state of loading to be seen at a glance and ejection can be changed from right to left merely by replacing the bolt and exposing the appropriate ejection port.

Made by Steyr-Daimler-Puch AG and
    Steyr-Mannlicher GmbH, Steyr, Austria
Specification Combat rifle
    Data from manufacturer's manual,
    Army Universal Assault Rifle 'Steyr'...
    (c. 1980)
Calibre 5.56mm
Cartridge 5.56x45, rimless
Operation Gas, selective fire
Locking system Rotating bolt
Length 790mm (31.0in)
Weight 3.6kg (7.9lb) without magazine
Barrel 508mm (20.0in), 6 grooves,
    right-hand twist
Magazine 30-round detachable box
    (standard pattern)
Rate of fire 680–850rds/min
Muzzle velocity 970m/sec (3182ft/sec)
    with ball ammunition

FN FNC

The 5.56mm FNC assault rifle is used in Sweden and Indonesia as well as Belgium. This left-handed soldier runs the risk of being hit by ejected cases.

The FNC is a successor to the short-lived CAL, Fabrique Nationale's first and comparatively unsuccessful attempt to introduce a rifle chambering 5.56mm ammunition. The dropping-block action of the FAL was not perpetuated in the CAL, as tests had shown it to be unsuitable. A rotating bolt was substituted, but the CAL was plagued with extraction problems and even the FNC, developed in the mid-1970s, suffered teething troubles of its own. These were not satisfactorily overcome until 1980.

This delay allowed other 5.56mm designs to establish themselves worldwide, particularly the AR15/M16 ArmaLite series. However, in addition to service in Belgium, the FNC is issued in Sweden as the Ak-5 and in Indonesia, both countries making guns under licence. The guns have been sold on the commercial market under a variety of designations, though the system changed in 1980. The current infantry rifles, with a folding butt, are known as Models 0000 (rifled for SS109 ammunition) and 2000 (for M193); the short 'Para' patterns are numbered 6000 and 7000 respectively.

Made by FN Herstal SA, Herstal-lèz-Liège, Belgium
Specification Combat rifle
Data from manufacturer's handbook, *FN Carbine F.N.C. Calibre 5,56x45mm. Operator's Manual* (dated March 1982)
Calibre 5.56mm
Cartridge 5.56x45, rimless
Operation Gas, selective fire
Locking system Rotating bolt
Length 997mm (39.25in*) butt extended
Weight 3.80kg (8.38lb*) without magazine
Barrel 449mm (17.68in*) without flash suppressor, 6 grooves, right-hand twist
Magazine 30-round detachable box
Rate of fire 625–700rds/min
Muzzle velocity 915m/sec (3002ft/sec*) with SS109 ball ammunition

The breech of an early FNC prototype, showing its Hensoldt optical sight.

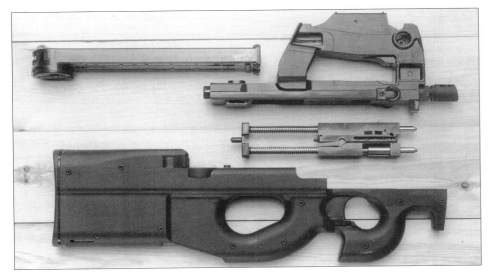

The 5.7mm FN P90® dismantled into its principal component groups. Note the unusual shape of the magazine, which incorporates a drum to turn the cartridges before they enter the breech.

The 'rifle' partner of the Five-seveN® pistol, this is an innovative design that challenges the popular infantry rifle preconceptions. Originally intended for issue to non-combatants, it is now being touted for much wider issue and has been adopted by nearly 20 armies worldwide. The weapon is exceptionally compact, with an ergonomic synthetic stock that stretches almost to the abbreviated muzzle. A transparent-bodied 50-round magazine lies on top of the receiver, embodying a drum that turns the cartridges before feeding them into the breech.

Open sights are duplicated on each side of a collimator unit and, as ejection is downward through the stock behind the pistol grip, the P90® is truly ambidextrous. The safety/selector is a radial catch beneath the trigger. The standard gun can be fitted with laser designators and light projectors and a suppressor can be attached to the muzzle. The P90® TR is a variant with a triple or Picatinny Rail and will accept most electro-optical and thermal-imaging sights.

Made by FN Herstal SA, Herstal-lèz-Liège, Belgium
Specification Non-combatant rifle
Data from Ian Hogg, *The Greenhill Military Small Arms Data Book* (1999) and the manufacturer's website, accessed August 2001
Calibre 5.7mm
Cartridge 5.7x28 P90®, rimless
Operation Recoil, selective fire
Locking system Not confirmed
Length 500mm (19.69in*)
Weight 3.0kg (6.61lb*) with loaded magazine
Barrel 263mm (10.35in), 8 grooves, right-hand twist
Magazine 50-round detachable box
Rate of fire 900rds/min
Muzzle velocity 715m/sec (2345ft/sec) with ball ammunition

The 5.56mm British L85A1 rifle fitted with a Rank Pullin SS80 Night Weapon Sight.

The saga of this gun has been repeated many times and it has attracted more than its share of controversy. The bullpup design is comparatively conventional, gas operated with a rotating-bolt locking system and the 4x SUSAT optical sight has undoubtedly improved the standard of shooting in the British Army. Unfortunately, the enforced change from 4.85mm chambering of the prototypes to 5.56x45 seems to have done nothing for efficiency and the standards of manufacture, and possibly also the choice of material, have been so poor that the catalogue of parts breakages seems never-ending.

Though remedial action has been taken, the problems that have led to the withdrawal of the L86A1 Light Support Weapon seem likely to account also for the Individual Weapon. It is notable that the SAS and British Commando units, who have more say in the choice of their personal weapons than the rank-and-file infantry, customarily favour the AR15/M16 series at the expense of the L85A1.

Made by Royal Ordnance plc, Nottingham, England
Specification Combat rifle
Data from Royal Ordnance leaflet, *Enfield Weapon System* (dated March 1985)
Calibre 5.56mm
Cartridge 5.56x45, rimless
Operation Gas, selective fire
Locking system Rotating bolt
Length 785mm (30.91in*)
Weight 3.80kg (8.38lb*) without magazine
Barrel 518mm (20.40in*), 6 grooves, right-hand twist
Magazine 30-round detachable box
Rate of fire 650–800rds/min*
Muzzle velocity 940m/sec (3084ft/sec*) with M193 ball ammunition

FA-MAS G2 France

The French service rifle, nicknamed *le Clairon* (the Bugle), is another that has had its share of detractors, concerned that its delayed-blowback action, relying on pivoting levers that connect the bolt and the bolt carrier, is only just strong enough to withstand firing the 5.56x45 cartridge.

However, the FA-MAS is popular with the troops, partly because it can readily be altered for left-handed marksmen simply by moving the extractor and closing the appropriate ejection port. The basic design has recently been upgraded from G1 to G2 standards by strengthening the recoil buffer, enlarging the trigger guard and adding a lipped fore-end to prevent the firer's supporting hand slipping in front of the muzzle. In addition, the magazine housing has been redesigned to NATO standards and can accept M16 and other magazines.

The French have also developed a compromise rifling, making a turn in 228mm (8.97in), which can fire M193 and SS109 ball ammunition without notable loss of accuracy.

Made by Manufacture d'Armes de Saint-Étienne (now part of GIAT)
Specification Combat rifle
  Data from Ian Hogg, *The Greenhill Military Small Arms Data Book* (1999)
Calibre 5.56mm
Cartridge 5.56x45, rimless
Operation Delayed blowback, selective fire
Locking system Inertia of two-part bolt/carrier unit
Length 757mm (29.8in)
Weight 3.7kg* (8.16lb*) with bipod and empty magazine
Barrel 488mm (19.20in), 3 grooves, right-hand twist
Magazine 30-round detachable box
Rate of fire 900–1000rds/min
Muzzle velocity 960m/sec (3150ft/sec) with M193 ball ammunition

A French FA MAS G1 rifle with a laser designator, used in conjunction with TN2-1 night observation goggles.

Heckler & Koch G3 Germany

The G3 derives from the Spanish CETME, developed in the early 1950s, which was itself based on design work undertaken in the Mauser factory towards the end of the Second World War.

Rollers between the bolt head and the bolt body, which must be pushed inward before the breech can open, provide sufficient delay to allow the chamber pressure to drop to a safe level – though the G3 has a reputation for harsh extraction even though the chamber is fluted. Many rifles remain in service in Germany, Denmark, Pakistan and Turkey. The basic design has been made as a submachine gun (MP5), in 5.56x45 (HK33, G41), as a light machine-gun and in sniping rifle forms (PSG-1, MSG90).

The basic rifle is easily recognised by its external appearance, but has been subjected to changes during its life. The most obvious has been the steady improvement of the pistol grip/selector unit, originally a metal pressing but synthetic on later guns. The standard G3 has a three-position selector (safe, single shot and fully automatic), originally marked either 'S', 'E' and 'F', or 'S', '1' and '20'; multiple-bullet symbols were then substituted and a three-round burst capability could be either added or substituted for the fully automatic option. These changes are reflected in the selector markings.

Another good feature of the G3A3 and its successors was the introduction of a sturdy backsight in the form of a small drum rotating on an axis that is more vertical than horizontal. This *Drehvisier*, with four sighting positions, has since been adapted by several other manufacturers.

Made by Heckler & Koch GmbH, Oberndorf/Neckar, Germany

Specification Combat rifle
Data from manufacturer's manual, *Brief Description of the Automatic Rifle* G3 (dated August 1983)
Calibre 7.62mm
Cartridge 7.62x51, rimless
Operation Delayed blowback, selective fire
Locking system Rollers on the bolt
Length 1025mm (40.68in)
Weight 4.4kg (9.68lb) without magazine
Barrel 450mm (17.71in), 4 grooves, right-hand twist
Magazine 20-round detachable box
Rate of fire 500–600rds/min
Muzzle velocity 790m/sec* (2592ft/sec*) with SS77 ball ammunition

A 7.62mm G3 with Heckler & Koch's HK79 single-shot grenade launcher replacing the standard fore-end. This gun has 'numbered' selector marks.

The culmination of trials dating back to the 1970s, the AR70/90 was approved as the new service rifle of the Italian armed forces in 1990 (though earlier versions have served Italian NOCS and GIS special forces for some years). The Beretta is a conventional design, with a rotating bolt, that embodies a large number of stamped and pressed parts. Translating the design from prototypes to a properly engineered series-made form has presented problems, one of the major changes made in the AR70/90 compared with the preceding AR70 and AR70/84 being the addition of hardened steel rails in the frame to

support the bolt. This was necessary to achieve reliability targets set on behalf of the army.

The rifle can be recognised by the detachable carrying handle/sight rail above the receiver, which can be pivoted sideways when required. The standard infantry version (AR) has a fixed polycarbonate butt, whereas the standard 'carbine' (SC) has a tubular butt that can fold forward along the right side of the receiver. Short-barrel versions are also made, including a paratroop carbine (SCP).

Made by Fabbrica d'Armi Pietro Beretta
    SpA, Gardone V.T. (Brescia), Italy
Specification Combat rifle
    Data from Ian Hogg, *The Greenhill*
    Military Small Arms Data Book (1999)
Calibre 5.56mm
Cartridge 5.56x45, rimless
Operation Gas, selective fire
Locking system Rotating bolt
Length 995mm (39.17in*)
Weight 3.94kg (8.69lb*) without magazine
Barrel 450mm (17.72in), 6 grooves,
    right-hand twist
Magazine 30-round detachable box
Rate of fire 600–650rds/min
Muzzle velocity 930m/sec (3051ft/sec*)
    with M193 ball ammunition

The 5.56mm Beretta AR70/90.

AK74M

The AK74M is the current version of the original AK47, developed immediately after the end of the Second World War, which has inspired a vast number of 5.45mm, 5.56mm, 7.62mm and 7.9mm adaptations and remains the rifle most likely to be found in the hands of insurgents and guerrillas. The AK74 was the first to introduce the 5.45x39 cartridge, which is still the regulation service round in Russia.

Unlike the AK74, which was made in fixed and folding-butt patterns, the 'M' version is designed for universal issue and has a synthetic butt that can be swung forward alongside the receiver. The fore-end and pistol grip are also durable plastic and a rail on the left sight of the receiver can accept optical and electro-optical sights when required.

The decision is said to have been taken to replace the Kalashnikov in Russian service with the Nikonov rifle (AN94) when funds permit, but the older design is still being made in quantity in Izhevsk and has laid the basis for the 'Hundred Series' guns currently being offered commercially.

Made by Izhmashzavod ('Izhevsk machinery factory'), Izhevsk, Russia

Specification Combat rifle
Data from John Walter, *Modern Military Rifles* (2001)
Calibre 5.45mm
Cartridge 5.45x39 M74, rimless
Operation Gas, selective fire
Locking system Rotating bolt
Length 956mm (37.64in)

Weight 4.85kg (10.69lb) with loaded 30-round magazine
Barrel 415mm (16.34in), 4 grooves, right-hand twist
Magazine 30-round detachable box (standard pattern)
Rate of fire 620–680rds/min
Muzzle velocity 900m/sec (2953ft/sec) with B-74 ball ammunition

The current version of the AK74M, from an Izhmashzavod leaflet.

CETME Modelo L

An optically sighted 5.56mm CETME Modelo L assault rifle in the hands of a member of the Spanish GEOS.

Derived from the 7.62x51 CETME series, and thus sharing common ancestry with the Heckler & Koch G3, this rifle retains the roller-delayed breech of the larger-calibre weapons. The Modelo L was adopted by the Spanish Army in 1987 and has since proved popular with special forces.

Incorporating more synthetic components than its German equivalent, the now-discontinued G41, the Modelo L has a drum-type backsight, though this has been changed for a simpler two-position rocking-leaf on the L1 variant. A compact LC is also made, with a barrel measuring just 320mm (12.6in). The pistol grip and the butt are moulded in a single piece; the trigger guard is generous enough to admit a thickly gloved finger; and the radial selector may have an additional burst-firing position, though this has now been reduced to the status of an optional extra.

Made by Empresa Nacional de Militares
   Santa Barbara, Oviedo, Spain
Specification Combat rifle
   Data from Ian Hogg, *The Greenhill Military Small Arms Data Book* (1999)
Calibre 5.56mm
Cartridge 5.56x45, rimless
Operation Gas, selective fire
Locking system Rollers on the bolt
Length 927mm* (36.5in)
Weight 3.42kg* (7.55lb) with empty magazine
Barrel 400mm* (15.75in), 6 grooves, right-hand twist
Magazine 30-round detachable box
Rate of fire 700–800rds/min
Muzzle velocity 969m/sec* (3180ft/sec) with SS109 ball ammunition

A variant of the Swiss Stg 90, the SG 551SP with a 16in barrel permitted by the US Bureau of Alcohol, Tax and Firearms.

The first 5.56mm rifle to be made by SIG, the SG 530, attempted to retain the roller-locking system pioneered by the Stgw 57 (SG 510). Unfortunately, the SG 530 never performed as well as its promoters had hoped and a rotating-bolt lock was substituted in the SG 540 series. These guns were successful enough for production to be licensed to Matra-Manurhin in France, tens of thousands of rifles being made in Mulhouse. Some of these were issued to French special forces and others were exported.

Trials in Switzerland proceeded so leisurely that the SG 540 metamorphosed into the 550 series before a decision to adopt the SG 550 (rifle) and SG 551 (carbine or 'headquarters weapon') was finally taken by the Swiss government in 1984. Issues of the *Sturmgewehr 90* were

completed by 1996, allowing the ageing Stgw 57 to be withdrawn into store.

The SG 550 and SG 551 are conventional rifles, differing only in length. Among the most obvious characteristics are the drum sights on the receiver, the diagonal void in the butt, and the transparent magazines. The incorporation of clips allows, for example, three 20-round magazines to be joined together, giving more firepower than a single 30-round unit and also allowing the firer to get closer to the ground when firing prone.

Made by SIG (Schweizerische Industrie-Gesellschaft), Neuhausen/Rheinfalls, Switzerland

Specification Combat rifle
Data from Swiss army handbook *Das Sturmgewehr 90. Bedienungsanleitung, Wf. 50.222* (February 1984 edition)
Calibre 5.56mm
Cartridge 5.56x45, rimless
Operation Gas, selective fire
Locking system Rotating bolt
Length 1000mm (39.37in*) butt extended
Weight 4.345kg (9.58lb*) with bipod and loaded 20-round magazine
Barrel 528mm (20.79in*), 6 grooves, right-hand twist
Magazine 20- or 30-round detachable box
Rate of fire 600–900rds/min
Muzzle velocity 980m/sec (3215ft/sec*) with M193 ball ammunition

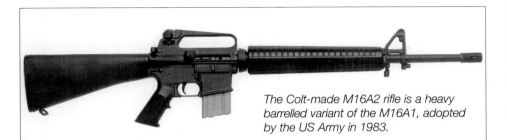

The Colt-made M16A2 rifle is a heavy barrelled variant of the M16A1, adopted by the US Army in 1983.

The story of the development of the ArmaLite AR15 and the chequered early history of the M16 in US service has been told on many occasions. However, once the teething troubles had been overcome, the M16 and its successors developed into the battleworthy weapons that have been proven throughout the world.

The original M16, retained for many years by the USAF, is the simplest of the series; a manual bolt-closing system was added to create the M16A1, regarded by many as an unnecessary complication; and Colt, the principal manufacturer, has offered commercially a range of sporting/military guns. The current variant, the M16A2, adopted in November 1983, was developed for the Marine Corps before being accepted for

universal service. The weight of the barrel was increased in an attempt to improve shooting, the backsight was improved and the butt was filled with nylon foam. Redesign enabled the flash-suppressor to double as a muzzle brake. Most guns have a three-round burst firing capability instead of the original fully automatic provision.

ArmaLite-type rifles have been made elsewhere, including Canada, the Philippines and Singapore, and have been used by many military, paramilitary and police units worldwide; the SAS, for example, customarily issues M16-type rifles instead of the ineffectual L85A1. The modern ArmaLite has few problems, excepting that the guns can be disabled if the butt, which contains the return spring,

breaks. Special forces will often use short-barrelled CAR-15 derivatives in preference to the infantry rifles, owing to their telescoping tubular steel butts.

Made by Colt's Manufacturing Company, Inc., Hartford, Connecticut, USA
Specification Combat rifle
Data from Ian Hogg, *The Greenhill Military Small Arms Data Book* (1999)
Calibre 5.56mm
Cartridge 5.56x45, rimless
Operation Gas, selective fire
Locking system Rotating bolt
Length 1000mm (39.37in)
Weight 3.40kg (7.50lb*) without magazine
Barrel 508mm (20.0in), 6 grooves, right-hand twist
Magazine 30-round detachable box
Rate of fire 800rds/min
Muzzle velocity 948m/sec (3110ft/sec) with M193 ball ammunition

SNIPING RIFLES

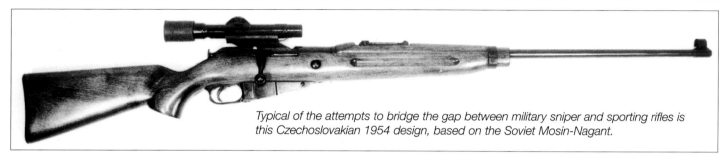

Typical of the attempts to bridge the gap between military sniper and sporting rifles is this Czechoslovakian 1954 design, based on the Soviet Mosin-Nagant.

The marksman has needs that are very different to his infantryman colleague, who depends more on firepower than pinpoint accuracy. Though the modern concept of sniping has a lengthy pedigree in military service, dating back before the American Civil War (1861–5) and was used to good effect in two world wars, only in recent years has the basic firearm progressed from a specially selected optically sighted service rifle.

More developmental effort has been put into sniping rifle design in the last 30 years than the preceding 300, but the financial investment has not been matched by gains in accuracy. A marksman from the First World War armed with a specially selected Canadian Ross rifle and selected .303

ammunition could probably outshoot many of today's specialist 7.62x51 'shooting kits'. However, there has been such a tremendous advance in sighting equipment that this comparison could scarcely be valid under anything but ideal daylight conditions. And the combat performance of a sniper depends as much on the firer's nerve and temperament as on his marksmanship.

The gun must be strong and durable enough to withstand active service. The traditional sniping rifle, being essentially a service pattern, was always more durable than its optical sights. However, the needs of many modern police and counter-terrorist agencies are less strenuous than a pre-1918 trenchscape and the role of

the sniper may often be combined with observation or intelligence gathering. This has led to the addition of features such as bipods and even the butt monopods that would once have been deemed inappropriate. However, the purchasers of military sniping rifles still often put durability before ultimate long-range accuracy and, until very recently, have been reluctant to issue anything other than regulation ammunition: 5.56x45 or 7.62x51 (NATO) or 7.62x54R (Warsaw Pact/Russia). Though many modern sniping rifles have trigger systems adapted from target rifles, these rarely make the leap from police to military usage. One exception is the Heckler & Koch MSG-90, which now shares the trigger unit of the PSG-1, but even this once had a simple refinement of the original military mass-issue G3 pattern!

The gun must contain as few parts as possible. This is true of any rifle, as long as it does not compromise function. The particular role of sniping rifles means that although simplicity is desirable, the sophistication of sights and trigger system may be deemed of greater value.

The gun must be easy to make and economical in terms of materials.

Sniping rifles are only purchased in small numbers and are, therefore, less affected by financial constraints that may restrict acquisitions of infantry weapons. Accuracy depends greatly on precise manufacture and this cannot be guaranteed if compromises are made in design or materials. The most accurate rifles tend to be those that originated as sporting/target guns.

The gun must be simple to operate and thus easily managed. Snipers are customarily better trained than rank and file and the need for simplicity is not paramount. However, a gun that is simpler to operate is undoubtedly better than one that is difficult to master. Consequently, although trigger systems, for example, may contain a multiplicity of parts, the basic functions and adjustments must be straightforward.

The gun must be as compact as possible. This is not as important in

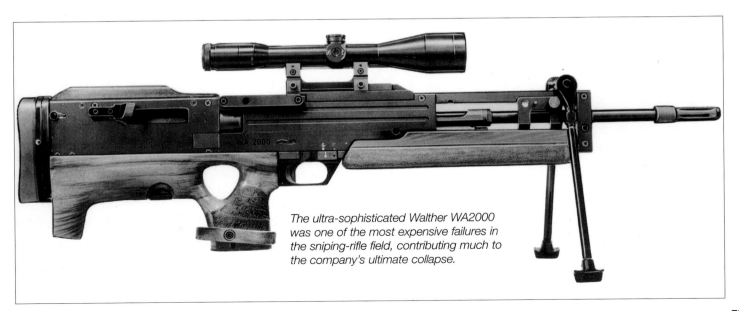

The ultra-sophisticated Walther WA2000 was one of the most expensive failures in the sniping-rifle field, contributing much to the company's ultimate collapse.

sniping-rifle design as in the case of mass-issue infantry weapons. The rifles must have barrels that are ballistically matched with the ammunition and, in the case of Magnum or long-range cartridges, this may mean barrel lengths of 65cm or more. However, additional weight makes the guns more stable, prevents muzzle whip and reduces the disturbance of a target picture if a second shot is needed. It is not uncommon for sniping rifles to weigh 6kg or more and the provision of bipods to support them is now regarded as standard procedure.

The gun must handle well. This criterion obviously applies to all weapons, sniping rifles included. Most modern designs are satisfactory, though military weapons – even though comb height and butt-plate length may be adjustable – must be designed to fit an 'average sniper'. Police weapons are often regarded in a more personal way, particularly in forces where there is latitude in the selection of equipment.

The gun must not jam in operation. This is vital in sniping and counter-sniping, where the first shot must count. Consequently, though semi-automatic rifles have been used in quantity by the US Army, in Germany and by the Soviet/Russian forces,

manually operated bolt-action rifles are usually preferred. These are usually quieter in operation than auto-loaders. Good quality ammunition, however, is another important limiting factor.

The gun must be easy to clean and simple to maintain. True in general terms, these considerations are not as important in sniping as in infantry weapons. Snipers are generally better trained, work more leisurely and do not always endure the same harsh service conditions as infantrymen.

The gun must be accurate, sufficiently powerful and offer sufficient range. This category is almost always a compromise. In the case of sniping equipment, however, it is of paramount importance. Consequently, even leading armies are prepared to countenance the issue of non-standard ammunition if it can improve first-hit performance. The new US Model 24 Remington Sniping System, a combination of the Model 40 target and Model 700 bolt-action sporting rifles, chambers the 7.62x51 NATO cartridge, but the specification insisted on an ability to change to .300 Winchester Magnum if long-term trials revealed improvements in accuracy. The Swedish Army PSG-90 sniping rifle, the British Accuracy International AW, can be chambered for the .338 Lapua

Magnum (8.6x70) cartridge compared with the 5.56x45 of the regulation Ak-5 (FN FNC).

The gun must carry as much ammunition as possible. This is unimportant in the context of sniping rifles, few of which have magazines for more than ten rounds. An exception is provided by 7.62x51 rifles such as the Heckler & Koch PSG-1 and MSG90, and the Swiss 5.56x45 SIG SSG 550, which can accept standard 20- or 30-round infantry-rifle magazines if necessary.

Details of only a few typical rifles are given here. Additional information can be found in another Greenhill Military Manual – Ian Hogg, *The World's Sniping Rifles* (2002).

Voere M2185SM Austria

The Voere M2185SM, a competition-grade auto-loader that can be pressed into sniping duties if required.

An interesting autoloading design introduced in the 1970s, this has been rebranded for military-match competition shooting. However, it is also typical of equipment that can be purchased from stock and simply pressed into a sniping role when required – whether by police or by terrorists – with minimal alteration. The rifle illustrated has a wood-laminate half-stock, with an adjustable comb and butt. It also has a Swarovski optical sight in a special one-piece mount on a receiver rail. The mount is allowed a small amount of controlled movement, to minimise the battering that can be transmitted to the sight by too rigid a fixing, without affecting zeroing.

Made by Voere Austria GmbH, Schwarzbach/Tirol, Austria
Specification Sniping rifle
Data from Ian Hogg, *The Greenhill Military Small Arms Data Book* (1999)
Calibre 7.62mm
Cartridge 7.62x51 NATO, rimless
Operation Gas, single shot only
Locking system Rotating bolt
Length 1165mm (45.87in)
Weight 3.450kg (7.61lb) with empty magazine
Barrel 520mm (20.47in), 4 grooves, right-hand twist
Magazine 5- or 10-round detachable box
Muzzle velocity 861m/sec (2825ft/sec) with ball ammunition

The Accuracy International AWS, with a full-length suppressor and a Schmidt & Bender optical sight.

Derived from the British L96A1 sniping rifle, this distinctive design has inspired developments elsewhere (e.g., the French Ultima Ratio® series and the abortive Mauser SR-93). The synthetic stock is made in two parts, bolted to a central aluminium chassis. This, and the ultra-stiff receiver, gives the AI design a rigidity lacking in many of its more traditionally made rivals, which are more susceptible to heat and humidity.

The straight-line configuration, thumbhole grip and adjustable butt plate improve control, directing recoil straight back into the firer's shoulder with minimal disturbance of the sight picture. The bolt is a short-throw three-lug type,

locking directly into the barrel behind the chamber; the trigger is adjustable; and a three-position safety catch can be set to fire, to lock the firing mechanism but allow the bolt to open, or to immobilise the bolt entirely.

AW rifles are made in a variety of patterns and chamberings, including a Super Magnum variant, but the particular AWS has a full-length sound moderator and a 6x42 Mark 2 Schmidt & Bender optical sight in a one-piece mount.

Made by Accuracy International Ltd, Portsmouth, Hampshire, England
Specification Sniping rifle
Data for standard AW rifle from Ian Hogg, *The World's Sniping Rifles* (2002)
Calibre 7.62mm
Cartridge 7.62x51 NATO, rimless
Operation Manual, single shot only
Locking system Rotating bolt
Length 1180mm (46.46in)
Weight 6.10kg (13.40lb) with empty magazine
Barrel 650mm (25.6in), 6 grooves, right-hand twist
Magazine 10-round detachable box
Muzzle velocity 850m/sec (2788ft/sec) with ball ammunition

Parker-Hale M85

The Parker-Hale M85 was entered in the British Army sniping-rifle competition that led to the standardisation of the Accuracy International L96A1. However, the M85 performed creditably enough to be rated as 'fit for service' and has since been sold to military and police agencies throughout the world. The action is basically a Spanish Santa Barbara 1898-type Mauser bolt in a rigid heavyweight receiver. A detachable box magazine and a high-comb straight-line butt are standard, relying on spacers (the gun pictured has four) to tailor the position of the butt plate to individual requirements. A hand-stop may be encountered beneath the fore-end, particularly on guns used for target shooting, but an adjustable bipod is customary on sniping rifles.

The Parker-Hale M85 sniping rifle, with a Rank Pullin SS80 Night Weapon Sight.

Made by Parker-Hale Ltd, Birmingham, England (prior to 1990), and by the Gibbs Rifle Company, Martinsburg, West Virginia, USA (since 1990)
Specification Sniping rifle
  Data from John Walter, *Rifles of the World* (second edition, 1998)
Calibre 7.62mm
Cartridge 7.62x51 NATO, rimless
Operation Manual, single shot only

Locking system Rotating bolt
Length 1149mm* (45.25in)
Weight 6.237kg* (13.75lb) with bipod and empty magazine
Barrel 699mm* (27.5in), 4 grooves, right-hand twist
Magazine 10-round detachable box
Muzzle velocity 861m/sec* (2825ft/sec) with ball ammunition

Tikka Model 65 Master Finland

The Tikka M65 Master, with military-style stock, a fluted barrel and a muzzle weight.

Introduced c. 1983, this adaptation of Tikka biathlon rifles has been used in small numbers by police marksmen in northern Europe. Essentially a modified 1898-pattern Mauser, with the safety lug replaced by the bolt handle entering a deep seat, it represents a traditional design. However, the comb and the butt-plate lock bolts can be adjusted with Allen keys, the stock is synthetic Cycolac and the anatomical near-vertical pistol grip improves control.

The free-floating barrel is fluted, saving weight but retaining rigidity, and a muzzle weight or muzzle brake can be fitted. The magazine release catch lies inside the trigger guard, ahead of the trigger lever, and a radial safety catch will be found on the right side of the receiver directly behind the bolt handle.

Made by Oy Tikkakoski Ab, Tikkakoski, Finland (part of Sako-Valmet Oy after 1989)
Specification Sniping rifle
Data from a manufacturer's catalogue, c. 1985
Calibre 7.62mm
Cartridge 7.62x51 NATO, rimless
Operation Manual, single shot only
Locking system Rotating bolt
Length 1175mm (46.26in) including muzzle weight

Weight 4.575kg (10.09lb) without magazine or sights
Barrel 650mm (25.59in), 6 grooves, right-hand twist
Magazine 10-round detachable box
Muzzle velocity 861m/sec (2825ft/sec) with ball ammunition

Blaser M93 Marksman Germany

An adaptation of a target rifle, this represents a departure from traditional practice. The proprietary bolt system consists of a rotating multi-segment collar that engages a shoulder in the barrel and can slide back on rails on top of the receiver after the action has been opened. The trigger mechanism lacks a conventional sear, working instead on a toggle principle.

The receiver is prolonged to form the fore-end and the butt. The comb and the butt plate can be adjusted to suit individual requirements, a bipod is attached beneath the fore-end and, in this particular case, a fixed-power optical sight with integral bullet-impact control drums is attached in a rigid one-piece mount. The barrel is fluted, combining light weight and rigidity. Guns of this type are expensive, but have nonetheless been tested (usually with a blacked finish) by police marksmen in Germany and Switzerland.

The Blaser M93 Marksman is typical of the high-quality target guns that can double as a sniper's rifle.

Made by W. Blaser GmbH, Isny/Allgau, Germany

Specification Sniping rifle
  Data from manufacturer's website, accessed in August 2001
Calibre 7.62mm
Cartridge 7.62x51 NATO, rimless
Operation Manual, single shot only
Locking system Rotating bolt
Length 1130mm* (44.5in*)
Weight 5.3kg (11.6lb) with empty magazine
Barrel 600mm (23.6in), 6 grooves, right-hand twist
Magazine 5- or 10-round detachable box
Muzzle velocity 850m/sec (2789ft/sec) with SS77 ball ammunition

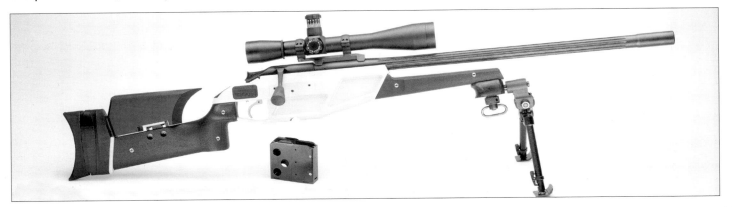

The IMI Hadar II, a derivative of the Galil, is intended primarily for police duties.

This is a semiautomatic version of the Galil service rifle, an adaptation of the Kalashnikov, set in a wooden thumbhole-type half stock. Intended for police use, the Hadar II has a safety-catch lever (safe/fire) on the left side of the pistol grip and a restricted-capacity box magazine released by a catch ahead of the trigger guard. Swivels lie on the 'steps' beneath the fore-end and on the underside of the butt, which has a ventilated rubber shoulder pad. Standard open sights can be fitted if required, but most purchasers prefer optical sights. This gun has an Israeli-made Nimrod 6x40 pattern in a one-piece mount.

Made by Israeli Military Industries (IMI), Ramat ha-Sharon, Israel

Specification Sniping rifle
Data from a manufacturer's leaflet (*c.* 1988)

Calibre 7.62mm

Cartridge 7.62x51 NATO, rimless

Operation Gas, single shot only

Locking system Rotating bolt

Length 980mm (38.6in*)

Weight 4.350kg (9.6lb*) with empty magazine

Barrel 450mm (17.7in*), 6 grooves, right-hand twist

Magazine 10-round detachable box

Muzzle velocity 850m/sec (2789ft/sec*) with SS77 ammunition

Tanner SSG Switzerland

Adapted from a target rifle, this is typical of the individualistic equipment that has been purchased by individual Swiss cantonal police units. The essence of the design lies in the sophisticated design of the bolt and the trigger mechanism and in the strength and rigidity of the massive receiver. A detachable box magazine is standard, the butt plate can be moved vertically and a system of replaceable combs can adapt to individual requirements. This particular gun has a 3–9x40 Swarovski telescope sight in a one-piece mount, but lacks the bipod that is often fitted to guns that may be required to double as observation aids.

Made by Werkstätte für Präzisionswaffe André Tanner, Fuhlenbach, Switzerland
Specification Sniping rifle
Data from manufacturer's leaflet, dated 1985
Calibre 7.62mm
Cartridge 7.62x51 NATO, rimless
Operation Manual, single shot only
Locking system Rotating bolt
Length 1150mm (45.28inin)
Weight 5.50kg (12.13lb) without sights
Barrel 660mm (25.98in), 4 grooves, right-hand twist
Magazine 10-round detachable box
Muzzle velocity 861m/sec (2825ft/sec) with SS77 ball ammunition

The Tanner Scharfschützengewehr, shown here with a Swarovski optical sight, derived from a UIT target rifle.

SIG-Sauer SSG 2000

Though now superseded by the SIG-Sauer 3000 (an adaptation of the Sauer Model 200 sporting rifle), this has proved popular with police and paramilitary units. Also offered in .223 (5.56x45), 7.5x55 Swiss and 7.62x51 NATO, it is essentially a militarised Sauer Model 80 rifle, sharing the same wedge-lock bolt, but has a detachable box magazine. The thumbhole-grip stock has a elevating comb and a adjustable butt plate, and a rail for accessories – such as a hand-stop, a sling anchor or a bipod – let into the underside of the fore-end. A sliding safety catch on the upper tang, immediately behind the bolt, displays the letter 'S' when set to its safety position, but an interlock stud on top of the bolt-handle base must be pressed before the bolt can open. The action incorporates a set trigger, which is activated by pushing the tip of the trigger forward once the safety has been set to 'S'; de-cocking is simply a matter of pressing the trigger with the safety catch applied. A signal pin protrudes from the left side of the receiver when a cartridge has entered the chamber and a cocking indicator can be seen beneath the tail of the bolt.

Guns may be fitted with accessories such as muzzle brake/compensators and mirage bands, and the sights are almost always optical. A fixed-power Zeiss Diatal ZA 8x56T sight can be fitted, but SIG also considered the 1.5–6x42 range-drum Schmidt & Bender design to be standard. A multi-adjustable Loga-system tripod, which could be attached to the fore-end rail or fitted with a padded fork when required, was also amongst the accessories.

Made by J.P. Sauer & Sohn GmbH, Eckenforde/Holstein, Germany, in collaboration with SIG (Schweizerische Industrie-Gesellschaft), Neuhausen/Rheinfalls, Switzerland

Specification Sniping rifle
Data from manufacturers' handbook, *SIG-Sauer SSG2000. Anleitung. Manual, Instructions* (c. 1985)
Calibre .300
Cartridge .300 Weatherby Magnum
Operation Manual, single shot only
Locking system Non-rotating bolt
Length 1260mm (49.61in*)
Weight 6.1kg (13.45lb*) with empty magazine
Barrel 660mm (25.98in*) excluding flash suppressor, 6 grooves, right-hand twist
Magazine 4-round detachable box
Muzzle velocity 990m/sec (3248ft/sec*) with ball ammunition

An exploded-view drawing of the SIG-Sauer SSG 2000.

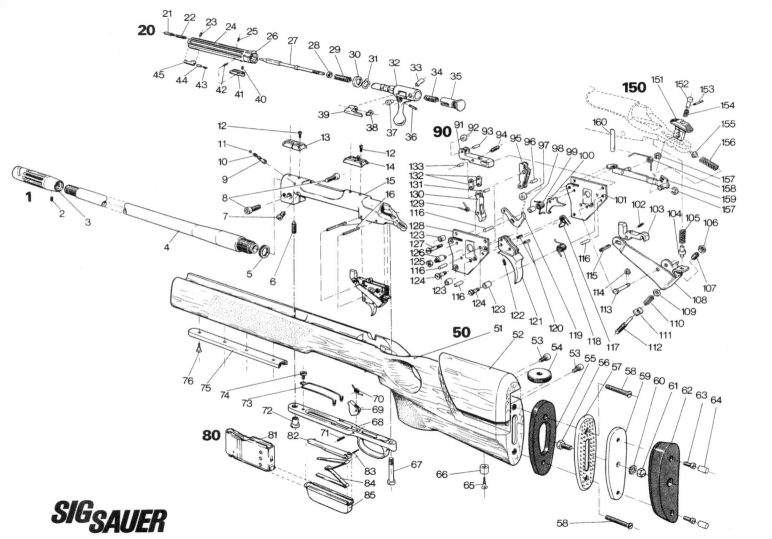

20

150

90

50

80

SIG SAUER

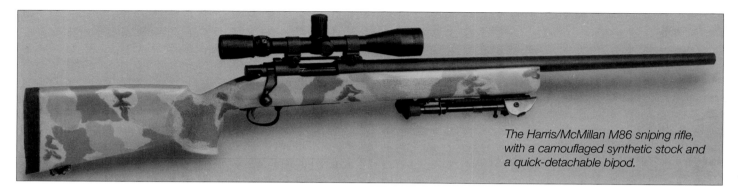

The Harris/McMillan M86 sniping rifle, with a camouflaged synthetic stock and a quick-detachable bipod.

This is typical of the purpose-built equipment available in North America, combining a modified Mauser action with a heavy barrel, matt-finish metalwork and a synthetic half-stock finished with a disruptive camouflage pattern. The essence of this particular design, contrasting with many of the ultra-sophisticated European approaches (e.g., SIG-Sauer SSG 2000), is to provide a reliable gun that can survive rough treatment with minimal attention. Consequently, the comb and butt plate are fixed, stippling is used on the pistol-grip and fore-end in preference to chequering and a detachable bipod is fitted beneath the fore-end. This particular rifle has a fixed-power optical sight with an illuminable reticle and computing range-drums, but the choice is usually left to the purchaser.

Made by Harris Gunworks, Inc., Phoenix, Arizona, USA

Specification Sniping rifle
Data from Ian Hogg, *The Greenhill Military Small Arms Data Book* (1999)

Calibre 7.62mm

Cartridge 7.62x51 NATO (.308 Winchester), rimless

Operation Manual, single shot only

Locking system Rotating bolt

Length 1105mm* (43.50in)

Weight 5.105kg* (11.25lb) with empty magazine

Barrel 610mm* (24.00in), 4 grooves, right-hand twist

Magazine 4-round detachable box

Muzzle velocity 861m/sec (2825ft/sec) with SS77 ball ammunition

Savage Model 116FSS

The Savage Model 116FSS bolt-action rifle, developed for sporting use, can double as a sniping rifle. Note the matt black synthetic stock and non-reflective corrosion resisting stainless-steel construction.

This typifies the type of all-purpose sporting rifle that can be purchased off the shelf yet still perform adequately as a sniping rifle. Remington, Ruger and Winchester all offer 'police' variants of their bolt-action rifles, customarily with plain finish and a variety of synthetic stocks, even though the basic designs may be 50 years old.

Savage makes a Model 110FP Tactical rifle, with a heavy barrel, non-reflective finish and a graphite/fibreglass half-stock with a proprietary pillar-bedding system. However, the Savage 116FSS (internal magazine) and 116FCS (detachable box magazine) sporting rifles fall into the same category. Light enough to be carried without fatigue, their durability is assured by a combination of a fibreglass-reinforced stock (F) and a matt-finish stainless-steel (SS) action, and accuracy is enhanced by the free-floating barrel. Optical-sight mounts can be attached to the receiver, no open sights being provided.

Made by Savage Arms, Inc., Westfield, Massachusetts, USA
Specification Sniping rifle
Data from Ian Hogg, *The Greenhill Military Small Arms Data Book* (1999)
Calibre 7.62mm
Cartridge 7.62x51 NATO (.308 Winchester), rimless
Operation Manual, single shot only
Locking system Rotating bolt
Length 1105mm* (43.50in)
Weight 2.950kg* (6.50lb) empty, without sights
Barrel 559mm* (22.00in), 4 grooves, right-hand twist
Magazine 4-round internal box
Muzzle velocity 861m/sec (2825ft/sec) with SS77 ball ammunition

The Yugoslavian M76 sniping rifle, chambered for the 7.9mm Mauser cartridge, is essentially a long-barrelled Kalashnikov.

The standard Soviet-bloc sniping rifle was the SVD (Dragunov), a purpose-built derivative of the Kalashnikov which is still being made in quantity in Russia, Romania and China. However, some countries on the fringe of the Warsaw Pact, such as Yugoslavia, have preferred rifles that are simply versions of the indigenous Kalashnikovs with heavier barrels and better sights. The Kragujevač-made M76 – chambered in this case for the 7.9x57 Mauser round – is typical of these attempts, as a comparison with a standard AKM/AK-74 will testify. The selector on the right side of the receiver is restricted to two positions (safe and single shot), the pistol grip and the butt have been refined and a heavyweight barrel has been fitted with a muzzle brake/compensator. Interestingly, the rifle will still accept the standard knife bayonet if required. The rifle pictured has a massive first-generation intensifying sight mounted on a rail attached to the left side of the receiver.

Made by Zavodi Crvena Zastava, Kragujevač, Yugoslavia (Serbia)
Specification Sniping rifle
Data from John Walter, *Kalashnikov* (2002)
Calibre 7.9mm
Cartridge 7.9x57 Mauser, rimless
Operation Gas, single shot only
Locking system Rotating bolt
Length 1135mm (44.69in*)
Weight 4.50kg (9.92lb*) without magazine and sights
Barrel 550mm (21.65in*), 4 grooves, right-hand twist
Magazine 10-round detachable box
Muzzle velocity 850m/sec (2789ft/sec*) with ball ammunition

Anti-matériel rifles

The continual quest to extend the range of sniping rifles has revived interest in these guns, essentially derivations of the anti-tank rifles fashionable in the 1918–45 era, but long since abandoned. The smallest guns are essentially enlargements of existing rifle-calibre weapons, but the largest owe more to heavy machine-guns and anti-tank rifles such as the Soviet PTRD (Degtyarev) of 1941.

Their popularity is easy to understand in view of their long-range striking power, which can be enough to destroy a vehicle or bring down a helicopter costing millions of dollars with a single inexpensive shot.

Most AMRs chamber either the .50 Browning (preferred by NATO) or the Soviet/Russian 12.7x108 and 14.5x114 machine-gun round, though attempts have been made to develop not only proprietary ammunition but also guns handling adapted 20mm cannon rounds.

The arbiter for this book is portability and only a few 20mm guns that can be considered as 'one man' have been included. Details of others will be found in two other Greenhill Military Manuals by Ian Hogg: *Small Arms: Pistols and Rifles* (2001) and *The World's Sniping Rifles* (2002).

The French PSM Hecate II anti-matériel rifle chambers the .50 Browning machine-gun cartridge.

This is an enlargement of the PSM Ultima Ratio® series of 7.62mm sniping rifles, chambered for the Browning machine-gun cartridge. The bolt has three locking lugs, the trigger is a two-stage 'military style', the strength of construction matches the power of the cartridge and a substantial muzzle brake has been added. A bipod attached to the fore-end and a monopod beneath the detachable butt allow observation to be undertaken without the strain of supporting the rifle on the shoulder. The bolt handle can also be detached when required. A folding carrying handle lies close to the centre of gravity and optical sights are standard.

Made by PGM Précision SARL, La Chambre and Poisy, France
Specification Anti-matériel rifle
Data from Ian Hogg and John Weeks, *Military Small Arms of the Twentieth Century* (seventh edition, 2000)
Calibre 0.5in
Cartridge 12.7x99 Browning, rimless
Operation Manual, single shot only

Locking system Rotating bolt
Length 1380mm (54.33in) butt, 1140mm* (44.88in*) without butt
Weight 13.50kg (29.76lb*) with empty magazine
Barrel 700mm (27.56in), 8 grooves, right-hand twist
Magazine 7-round detachable box
Muzzle velocity 850m/sec (2788ft/sec) with ball ammunition

The breech of the 14.5mm Gepard M3, possibly the most powerful 'single-man' rifle currently available.

The Gepards are interesting minimalistic weapons, with a bolt sliding in an elongated tubular receiver that supports the barrel and ends in a massive shoulder pad.

The 12.7mm M1 and M1A1 are manually operated, whereas the auto-loading 12.7mm M2 and the 14.5mm M3 rely on long recoil. The M3 is perhaps the most powerful one-man gun currently available, though its great length and weight would restrict it only to the strongest.

The barrel and the bolt recoil for 13cm (5.1in), locked together, before the barrel is halted and the bolt rotates out of engagement. The bolt is then held back as the barrel returns, then follows to strip a new round into the chamber before the parts run back into battery and lock once again. The pistol grip lies alongside the detachable box magazine, restricting the Gepard to right-handed firers, and a bipod is attached to a collar around the receiver. A hinged lid covers the ejection port and a one-piece bracket for an optical sight can be attached to the receiver top.

Made by Technika NV, Budapest, Hungary
Specification Anti-matériel rifle Data from Ian Hogg, *The Greenhill Military Small Arms Data Book* (1999)
Calibre 0.5in
Cartridge 12.7x99 Browning, rimless
Operation Recoil, single shot only
Locking system Rotating bolt
Length 1880mm (74.0in)
Weight 20.0kg (44.1lb) without magazine
Barrel 1480mm (58.27in), 6 grooves, right-hand twist
Magazine 5- or 10-round detachable box
Muzzle velocity 1000m/sec (3280ft/sec) with ball ammunition

Barrett M82A1 Light Fifty

The Barrett Light Fifty. This example is an original M82, with a solid butt-web and handguard.

The first AMR to gain widespread acceptance, the Light Fifty has been used by US special forces and comparable units throughout the world, but has also achieved notoriety in the hands of the IRA.

An auto-loading design chambered for the Browning machine-gun cartridge, it offers straight-line configuration, a detachable box magazine and an M16-type pistol grip. A bipod is attached beneath the receiver casing, midway between the magazine and the tip of the fore-end, and there are now three lateral gas-escape ports on each side of the sturdy muzzle brake. Optical sights can be mounted on a rail, pierced with lightening holes, that has been welded to the top of the receiver.

The original M82 had a solid-side butt instead of a skeletal pattern, but was rapidly upgraded to M82A1 standards. The M82A2 is a bullpup variant, with an auxiliary fore-grip, and Barrett also offers a simpler bolt-action gun, the M90A1. This is merely 45in overall and weighs 22lb.

Made by Barrett Firearms Mfg Co., Murfreesboro, Tennessee, USA

Specification Anti-matériel rifle
Data from Ian Hogg, *The Greenhill Military Small Arms Data Book* (1999)
Calibre 0.5in
Cartridge 12.7x99 Browning, rimless
Operation Recoil, single shot only
Locking system Rotating bolt
Length 1447mm (57.0in)
Weight 12.90kg (28.44lb) with empty magazine
Barrel 737mm (29.00in), 8 grooves, right-hand twist
Magazine 10-round detachable box
Muzzle velocity 850m/sec (2789ft/sec) with ball ammunition

The Harris/McMillan M93 anti-matériel rifle.

Simply an enlargement of the standard Harris/McMillan sniping rifles, this derivative of the older M87 and M88R is a conventional-looking weapon, betrayed only by its size, elongated magazine and multi-port muzzle brake. The thumbhole butt – which can be folded sideways when required – and fore-end are fibreglass, separate butt units being provided to cater for individual preferences. A curved plate has been added to the left side of the butt to serve as a cheekpiece, the bipod is mounted on a spigot protruding from the fore-end – unlike on the M87, where it was set into the fore-end body – and a monopod beneath the pistol grip facilitates use of the rifle in an observation role. The gun illustrated has an optical sight attached to a rail above the receiver, with handy flip-up protective caps.

Made by Harris Gunworks, Inc., Phoenix, Arizona, USA

Specification Anti-matériel rifle
Data from Ian Hogg, *The Greenhill Military Small Arms Data Book* (1999)
Calibre 0.5in
Cartridge 12.7x99 Browning, rimless
Operation Manual, single shot only
Locking system Rotating bolt
Length 1346mm (53.00in)
Weight 9.75kg (21.5lb) with bipod and empty magazine, without sights
Barrel 737mm (29.00in), 8 grooves, right-hand twist
Magazine 5-round detachable box
Rate of fire NA
Muzzle velocity 850m/sec (2789ft/sec) with ball ammunition

LIGHT AUTOMATIC WEAPONS

Though handguns, shotguns and rifles satisfy many of the needs of special forces and police tactical firearms units, there are times when a greater volume of fire is required. On an individual basis, this can be provided by a submachine gun or a one-man light machine-gun, which may be nothing more than a heavy-barrelled rifle capable of firing fully automatically. On a crewed basis, the solutions can include sustained-fire machine-guns (SFMGs) and automatic grenade launchers.

Pinpoint accuracy is rarely a prerequisite of automatic weapons design, as the primary criterion is usually the ability to saturate a designated area with bullets. Any tendencies to spread the fall of shot, therefore, has been welcomed and very little attempt has been made to improve the accuracy of submachine guns, in particular, until recent years.

Guns such as the wartime British Sten, the German MP38/MP40 series and the Soviet PPSh were made in huge quantities, but accuracy was comparatively poor and the use of pistol ammunition restricted range. Post-war

guns such as the Uzi and the Ingram have continued this trend, the goals often being a reduction in size instead of improved performance. Consequently, though submachine guns were used by terrorists and counter-terrorism units alike – the Uzi, in particular, being issued widely – not until the Heckler &

Koch MP5 appeared was a change in design emphasis to be seen.

The MP5 retained the roller system of the G3 rifle and, firing from a closed bolt in single-shot mode, gave much better accuracy than any of its predecessors. This freed specialist units from the 'spray all' tendencies of

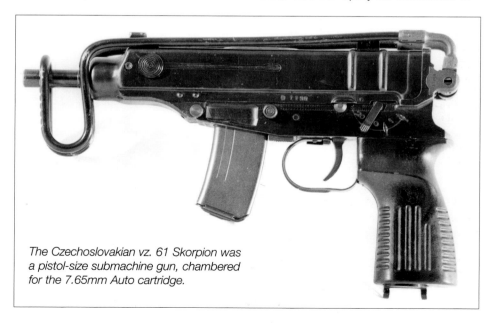

The Czechoslovakian vz. 61 Skorpion was a pistol-size submachine gun, chambered for the 7.65mm Auto cartridge.

conventional submachine guns, which could be damaging to hostages or property, by giving them the choice of accurate shot placement or concentrated continuous fire.

Attempts are still being made to provide ultra-simple designs, owing to the expense of incorporating a locked breech and a trend has recently been evident towards personal-defence weapons that are more like oversize pistols than traditional submachine guns. However, this is a route that has been travelled many times before (e.g., the Mauser *Schnellfeuerpistolen* of the 1930s or the Soviet APS of the 1950s) without ever encountering success, though the ultra-compact Czechoslovakian Scorpion, chambered for a variety of weak pistol rounds, was at least a qualified success.

Experiments have also been made to develop ammunition that is better suited to this role than the venerable 9x19 (Parabellum) or .45 ACP pistol rounds. FN Herstal SA has introduced a 5.7x28 round that seems likely to become a NATO standard and Heckler & Koch has produced a 4.6x30 pattern. These fire comparatively lightweight bullets at high velocity (730m/sec or more) and special subcalibre sabot projectiles have proved capable of defeating multiple layers of Kevlar body

The 5.56x45 Steyr AUG configured as a light support weapon, with heavy barrel, optical sight, carrying handle and a large-capacity magazine that hinders shooting prone from behind minimal cover.

armour and even a NATO-standard steel helmet at short range.

The MP5 is essentially an assault rifle in miniature, chambering pistol ammunition. Its success has encouraged other manufacturers, the most successful conversion being the Steyr AUG, which can be adapted to fire 9x19 cartridges simply by replacing the barrel and the bolt and inserting an adaptor in the magazine. The basic AUG can also be configured as a light machine-gun, with a heavy barrel mounting a carrying

handle and a bipod.

The idea of a one-man machine-gun stretches back prior to the First World War, with the advent of the Madsen. The widespread issue of the Lewis Gun, the Chauchat and eventually the Browning Automatic Rifle during the First World War allowed support fire to delivered during an assault in a way that the Maxim, Vickers and Browning water-cooled weapons could not match. The idea of portability was developed during the inter-war years, producing guns such as the ZB 26 and the Bren Gun and establishing the box magazine as ideal. The concept was developed even further by the Johnson light machine-gun of 1944, a quirky design that weighed less than 6kg, and then into the modern Light Support Weapon (LSW).

However, the limited capacity of a box magazine does not allow fire to be sustained and the fixed barrel (which heats up too rapidly) of some otherwise praiseworthy lightweight weapons is also a weakness. Today's designs answer these problems by accepting penalties of extra weight in return for strength, and sometimes by allowing belts or box magazines to be used interchangeably. It is no coincidence that the most popular guns in this class are the Belgian-designed Minimi and the Heckler & Koch patterns, each of which is sturdy enough to sustain fire from ammunition belts and light enough to perform as a heavy automatic rifle when fitted with box magazines. Indeed, the German police have used a semi-automatic variant of the HK21E machine-gun as a sniping rifle.

The gun must be strong and durable enough to withstand active service. Most modern automatic weapons are satisfactory, though the need to balance volume of fire with controllability and durability inevitably creates compromises.

The gun must contain as few parts as possible. A trend towards simplification has been evident in recent years, with the introduction of synthetic components. This is particularly true of submachine guns, where the goal is still the cheapest production commensurate with adequate performance, but is less obvious in the case of light machine-guns. The latter group customarily chamber rifle ammunition, requiring considerable strength to handle the pressures generated in the chamber and must be heavy enough to control when firing automatically. The need to duplicate the feed, so that belts or box magazines can be used, is also an inevitable complication.

The gun must be easy to make and economical in terms of materials. The introduction of synthetic components has often eased production problems, but the requirements for a submachine gun or a light machine-gun differ: the former, ideally, needs to be simple and inexpensive, whereas the latter needs to be durable and heavy enough to control.

The gun must be simple to operate and thus easily managed. Submachine guns have almost always been simple, often to the extent that safety was minimal. Modern designs require ambidextrous controls and proper safety features, adding to what is basically a very simple concept. However, the controls are usually easy to master. Light machine-guns are inevitably more complex, particularly those that have dual feed capabilities, detachable barrels and sophisticated mounts. Here, too, attempts – not always successful – have been made to simplify operation.

The gun must be as compact as possible. Attempts are still underway to reduce the size of submachine guns, in the form of the Steyr Tactical Machine Pistol (TMP) or the Heckler & Koch Personal Defence Weapon (PDW). There is no evidence that these will supersede the category represented by the perfected MP5, except in the hands of a few specialist agencies who need a truly automatic weapon that can be concealed with ease. Military thinking is currently focussing on mid-size weapons such as the FN P90® and simple pistols firing the same ammunition, restricting the classical submachine gun to specialists.

The gun must handle well. Ergonomics play a major part in modern design and modern guns usually handle satisfactorily. The duplication of key

Now discontinued, the Calico M100P was a praiseworthy attempt to provide a large-capacity helical-feed magazine within the dimensions of a large pistol.

controls is undoubtedly an asset.

The gun must not jam in operation. Modern submachine guns often perform better than their predecessors, as it is very rare for an MP5, for example, to jam. Light machine-guns, however, have always performed well; the Bren Gun, particularly the 7.62mm L4 series conversions, had such a reputation for flawless functioning that the replacement, the 5.56mm L86A1 LSW, was an exceptionally poor substitute. Gains in this particular class, therefore, are often due more to better features and advances in construction than performance.

The gun must be easy to clean and simple to maintain. Most modern designs pay attention to maintenance, though a blowback submachine gun is obviously far easier to strip than a dual-feed support weapon.

The gun must be accurate, sufficiently powerful and offer sufficient range. The trend towards cartridges such as FN's 5.7x28 type, which generates far higher velocity than the traditional 9x19 or .45 ACP pistol rounds, improves the performance of weapons the size of submachine guns. However, the long-range accuracy of 5.56x45 ammunition calls into question whether something is to be gained either by retaining the 7.62x51 NATO cartridge or developing an entirely new round that could be chambered in LSWs, SFMGs and sniping rifles alike. The compromise between bullet diameter, bullet weight, velocity and range remains difficult to resolve.

The gun must carry as much ammunition as possible. Submachine guns and light machine-guns may be limited by the size of their box magazines, which usually feed from beneath the receiver and often inhibit firing from the prone position if no cover is available. This is particularly true of the 42-round magazine for the AUG or the 40-round magazines of the RPK. The Soviet RPD fed from a short belt contained in a drum-like case, but the best answer is probably provided by the Minimi – which accepts its magazines at an angle.

Details of only a few typical weapons are given here. Additional information can be found in other Greenhill Military Manuals – Ian Hogg, *Submachine Guns* (2000), and John Walter, *Modern Machine-Guns* (2000).

AUG-SMG

Austria

The 9mm AUG submachine gun, showing the adaptor required for the smaller magazine. Current guns have a broader web between the rear of the adaptor body and the stock.

This is an interesting variant of the AUG assault rifle (q.v.), introduced in 1986, which can be converted to a submachine gun by replacing the 5.56mm barrel with a 9mm pattern, exchanging the rotating-bolt unit for a blowback mechanism, and inserting an adaptor in the magazine aperture. The special 9mm magazine boxes can then be inserted in the normal way.

The 9mm AUG retains the one-piece synthetic stock/grip unit, with a folding foregrip attached to the barrel and can be fitted with the standard 1.5x optical sight/carrying handle unit. Alternatively, a flat-top bracket will accept virtually any optical or electro-optical sight made to STANAG dimensions. An optional suppressor can be fitted to the barrel and, if necessary, rifle grenades can be launched.

Made by Steyr-Daimler-Puch AG and
  Steyr-Mannlicher GmbH, Steyr, Austria
Specification Submachine gun
  Data from Ian Hogg, *The Greenhill
  Military Small Arms Data Book* (1999)
Calibre 9mm
Cartridge 9x19, rimless
Operation Blowback, selective fire
Locking system None
Length 665mm (26.18in)

Weight 3.30kg (7.28lb*) with empty
  25-round magazine
Barrel 420mm (16.54in), 6 grooves,
  right-hand twist
Magazine 25- or 32-round detachable
  box
Rate of fire 700rds/min
Muzzle velocity 400m/sec (1312ft/sec)
  with ball ammunition

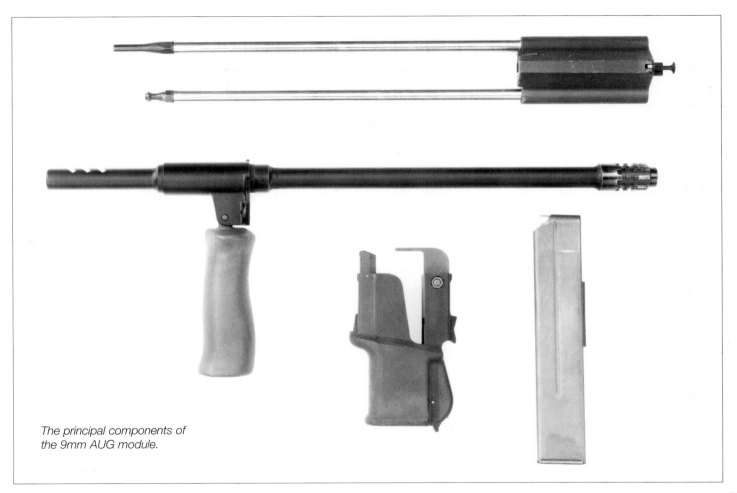

The principal components of the 9mm AUG module.

L2A3 Sterling

The British L2A3 Sterling submachine gun, shown here with a Rank Pullin SS82 weapon sight, was a traditional but surprisingly efficient performer.

Derived from the Patchett, developed at the end of the Second World War, the Sterling was adopted by the British Army in 1953 and saw front-line service until replaced in the 1990s by the 5.56mm L85A1. It is a conventional submachine gun design, made of steel and plastic and thus comparatively expensive. The butt folds downward.

The incorporation of rollers in the magazine, replacing the feed platform, and ribs machined on the bolt-body to expel fouling ensure a reputation for reliability; consequently, the Sterling was widely sold to military and police forces throughout the world and has only recently been overtaken in popularity in English-speaking areas by the Heckler & Koch MP5.

The semi-automatic L34A1, with an large-diameter integral silencer, has been used by the SAS and other specialist counter-terrorist units.

Made by Sterling Engineering Co. Ltd, Dagenham, Essex, England
Specification Submachine gun
Data from Ian Hogg, *The Greenhill Military Small Arms Data Book* (1999)
Calibre 9mm
Cartridge 9x19, rimless
Operation Blowback, automatic or selective fire
Locking system None
Length 690mm (27.17in) butt extended; 483mm (19.0in) with stock folded
Weight 2.72kg (6.0lb) with empty magazine
Barrel 198mm (7.80in), 6 grooves, right-hand twist
Magazine 34-round detachable box
Rate of fire 550rds/min
Muzzle velocity 390m/sec (1280ft/sec) with ball ammunition

Beretta M12S Italy

This compact design originated in the late 1950s, incorporating the then fashionable method of recessing the bolt head to receive the barrel. Popularised in Czechoslovakia and then featured in guns such as the Uzi, this shortened the action considerably. The M12 was introduced commercially in 1964, made largely of pressings and stampings, and can be recognised by the magazine protruding from a housing midway between the two pistol grips. The receiver has a knurled cap at each end, the selector lies on the left side of the frame immediately above the trigger, a cross-bolt locking catch for the grip safety is fitted and the metal butt folds to the right alongside the receiver.

The M12S, which appeared in the early 1980s, is an improved form of the M12. The selector was combined with the safety catch and redesigned to be ambidextrous, the design of the end-cap catch was improved, the sights were refined and the metal parts were coated

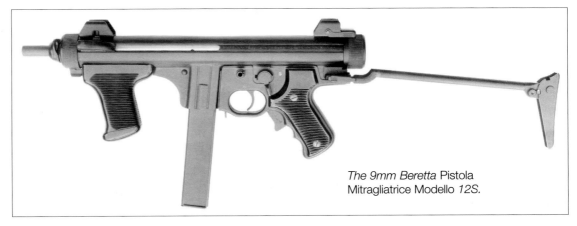

The 9mm Beretta Pistola Mitragliatrice Modello 12S.

with a protective coat of epoxy resin. Guns of this type have been used by Italian NOCS and GIS special forces and have also been made in quantity in Brazil by Forjas Taurus.

Made by Fabbrica d'Armi Pietro Beretta SpA, Gardone V.T. (Brescia), Italy
Specification Submachine gun
Data from Ian Hogg, *The Greenhill Military Small Arms Data Book* (1999)
Calibre 9mm
Cartridge 9x19, rimless
Operation Blowback, selective fire
Locking system None

Length 645mm (25.40in) butt extended; 417mm (16.43in) butt folded
Weight 3.0kg (6.56lb*) with empty magazine
Barrel 200mm (7.9in), 6 grooves, right-hand twist
Magazine 20-, 32 or 40-round detachable box
Rate of fire 550rds/min
Muzzle velocity about 380m/sec (1250ft/sec) with ball ammunition

The silenced (SD) version of the Heckler & Koch MP5.

The success of the MP5 has been due to its breech design, essentially the same as the G3 rifle, which gives an attractive combination of accuracy and reliability in a class of gun not known for these qualities. This suits the MP5 to military and police units involved in clandestine warfare or in sensitive urban areas (e.g., airports) where excessive cartridge power can be a liability.

The MP5 resembles an infantry rifle in miniature, its size betrayed most obviously by the narrow magazine; the markings on the selector follow conventional Heckler & Koch practice ('S', 'E' and 'F' on the oldest guns, multi-bullet illustrations on newer ones) and the material of the pistol grip/trigger housing group has gradually changed from pressed steel to synthetic injection moulding. The drum sight and the cocking handle in a tube above the left side of the fore-end are retained.

There have been many variants of the basic design, including the basic MP5A2 (fixed butt) and MP5A3 (telescoping butt). The MPA4, the current version, has ambidextrous controls and is generally supplied with a three-round burst firing capability. However, modular construction allows a variety of options to be supplied.

The MP5SD series has a large-diameter silencer instead of the conventional fore-end. The K-suffix guns are ultra-compact, the MP5KA5 measuring merely 325mm (12.8in) overall. The MP5K-PDW, developed in the USA, has a folding stock, an optional silencer and attachments for a laser designator or light projector. A 10mm variant was made in small numbers for the FBI in the 1980s, but H&K is now committed to investigating the 9x19 UMP *(Universal-Maschinen-Pistole)* and the gas-operated 4.6x30 PDW.

Made by Heckler & Koch GmbH, Oberndorf/Neckar, Germany

Specification Submachine gun
   Data from the manufacturer's website, accessed in August 2001
Calibre 9mm
Cartridge 9x19, rimless
Operation Delayed blowback, selective fire
Locking system Rollers on the bolt
Length 680mm (26.77in*)
Weight 2.54kg (5.60lb*) with empty magazine
Barrel 225mm (8.86in*), 4 grooves, right-hand twist
Magazine 15- or 30-round detachable box
Rate of fire 800rds/min
Muzzle velocity 400m/sec (1312ft/sec) with ball ammunition

The ultra-compact Heckler & Koch MP5KA4, with an additional burst-firing capability (note the four-position selector).

Light machine-guns

FN Minimi   Belgium

A prototype of the Belgian Minimi machine-gun, showing the box-magazine adaptor in place beneath the feedway for the belt.

The most successful of the current generation of light support weapons, currently being made in Australia, Korea and the USA in addition to Belgium, the gas-operated Minimi relies on a well-proven rotating bolt locking directly into the barrel extension. The chromed-bore barrel can be changed extremely easily, the assembly including the carrying handle, the gas-port block and the front sight.

Among the most unusual features of the design is its ability to handle metal-link belts or standard NATO-type box magazines, provided that an adaptor has been slotted into place beneath the feedway for the belt. The magazines point diagonally downward, reducing ground clearance.

The safety catch runs laterally through the frame above the pistol grip and a two-position selector on the gas port allows power to be adjusted to suit ammunition. Some guns are rifled for Belgian SS109 ball ammunition, some for the US M193 type and a few for a compromise pattern developed by the French. A sliding-butt version was developed for special purposes, but this has now been replaced by the Minimi-Para, with a short barrel and a two-tube sliding butt that rotates through 90° to stow alongside the receiver.

The US M249 Squad Automatic Weapon, made in Columbia, South Carolina, encountered teething troubles and was eventually superseded by the 'product improved' M249A1. This has an improved recoil buffer, a heat shield above the barrel, a fixed gas regulator and a folding carrying handle. The Australian F89 variant is essentially similar.

A production version of the Minimi (note the design of the butt and fore-end), with a Smith & Wesson Luna-Tron electro-optical sight.

Made by FN Herstal SA, Herstal-lèz-Liège, Belgium
Specification Light support weapon
Data from Ian Hogg, *The Greenhill Military Small Arms Data Book* (1999)
Calibre 5.56mm
Cartridge 5.56x45, rimless
Operation Gas, selective fire
Locking system Rotating bolt
Length 1040mm (40.94in)
Weight 6.83kg (15.06lb) with bipod
Barrel 466mm (18.35in), 6 grooves, right-hand twist
Feed 200-round metal-link belt or 30-round detachable box
Rate of fire 450–550rds/min
Muzzle velocity 925m/sec (3035ft/sec) with SS109 ball ammunition

Heckler & Koch HK21E

Germany

The current form of the HK21, introduced in the late 1960s, has an additional burst-firing capability, the barrel casing extended virtually to the muzzle and a commensurately extended sight radius. The pistol grip/trigger housing is now synthetic, usually with bullet symbols, although numbers are available to order, and the butt has a deepened belly to facilitate a second-hand hold.

One of the most interesting features of the HK21E, and the 5.56mm HK23E, lies in an ability to use box magazines if the appropriate adaptor has been substituted for the belt-feed tray unit. The barrel can be detached simply by lifting the locking handle and withdrawing it, breech first, from the open right side of the barrel casing. An auxiliary hand-grip can be fitted beneath the barrel casing and a buffered tripod mount is among the many accessories.

Guns of this type have been made under licence in Greece and Portugal as well as in Germany and a semi-automatic variant has been used by the German police as a sniping rifle.

Made by Heckler & Koch GmbH, Oberndorf/Neckar, Germany

Specification Light support weapon Data from Ian Hogg, *The Greenhill Military Small Arms Data Book* (1999)
Calibre 7.62mm
Cartridge 7.62x51 NATO, rimless
Operation Delayed blowback, selective fire
Locking system Rollers on the bolt
Length 1140mm (44.88in*)
Weight 9.30kg (20.50lb*) with bipod
Barrel 560mm (22.05in*), 4 grooves, right-hand twist
Feed Metal-link belt or 30-round detachable box
Rate of fire 800rds/min
Muzzle velocity 850m/sec (2789ft/sec*) with ball ammunition

A Heckler & Koch HK21E light machine-gun, with the old 'lettered' selector markings.

104

Negev Israel

A leading contender in the 'ideal LSW' category, this compact gas-operated design relies on twin return springs and a forked piston-rod to keep action length to a minimum. The gun is made of pressings, stampings and synthetic parts, keeping manufacturing complexity to a minimum, and can be easily field-stripped.

The butt folds to the left alongside the receiver, Galil-type open sights are fitted and a rail on the receiver top will accept optical and electro-optical sight mounts made to STANAG restrictions. The selector and the gas regulator each have three positions, tritium night sights can be provided and the Negev can be fitted to a tripod if required.

Its most interesting feature, however, is convertibility. Galil and M16 box magazines can be used if an adaptor has been fitted into the receiver beneath the feedway for the belt and the substitution of a short barrel allows the Negev to function as a compact assault rifle once the bipod has been detached.

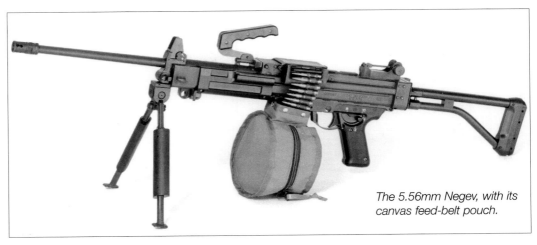

The 5.56mm Negev, with its canvas feed-belt pouch.

Made by Israeli Military Industries (IMI), Ramat ha-Sharon, Israel
Specification Light support weapon Data from an IMI handbook dated July 1988
Calibre 5.56mm
Cartridge 5.56x45, rimless
Operation Gas, selective fire
Locking system Rotating bolt
Length 1020mm (40.16in*) butt extended; 780mm (30.71in*) butt folded
Weight 7.2kg (15.87lb*) with bipod
Barrel 460mm (18.11in*), 6 grooves, right-hand twist

Feed Metal-link belt or detachable box
Rate of fire 650–850 or 750–950rds/min (selectable)
Muzzle velocity 950m/sec (3117ft/sec*) with M193 ball ammunition

Colt LMG M16A2

Also known as the Model 750 or LMG15, this is an adaptation of the US Army M16A2 assault rifle to serve as a light support weapon. Unlike the rifle, the machine-gun fires from the open bolt position and a bolt locking directly into the barrel extension keeps the weight of the receiver to a minimum. An improved hydraulic buffer reduces cyclic rate well below the excessive levels associated with the AR15/M16 rifle series, which often make the lightweight rifles difficult to control.

Customarily rifled with a twist of one turn in 7in (178mm), the LMG M16A2 is easily identified by the squared fore-end with prominent flutes and by the tubular fore-grip. The bipod, attached to the muzzle, is designed to be used with one hand. Standard US M16 and NATO-standard magazines may be used, although a high-capacity drum can also be obtained.

Made by Colt's Manufacturing Company, Inc., Hartford, Connecticut, USA
Specification Light support weapon
Data from an undated Colt catalogue sheet
Calibre 5.56mm
Cartridge 5.56x45, rimless
Operation Gas, automatic fire only
Locking system Rotating bolt
Length 1006mm* (39.60in)
Weight 5.78kg* (12.75lb) without magazine
Barrel 508mm* (20.0in), 6 grooves, right-hand twist
Magazine 30-round detachable box
Rate of fire 600–750rds/min
Muzzle velocity 991m/sec (3250ft/sec) with M193 ball ammunition

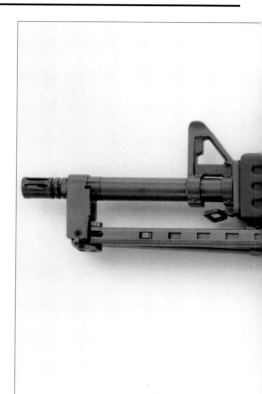

The Colt M16A2 LMG, showing box and drum magazines.

SIGHTS

Among the most indispensable items in the armoury of special forces are the observation tools and gunsights that enable an enemy to be observed in detail under the most daunting conditions. These include optical patterns, which are largely confined to daylight, and an array of infrared, image-intensifying, laser and thermal-imaging equipment that can facilitate observation in all but the blackest of nights.

The open sights of the 1990s include tangent-leaf sights of differing forms; and aperture or peep sights, ranging from the simplest battle pattern to micro-adjustable competition diopter sights with integral filters and adjustable irises.

Front sights still generally consist of a simple ramp-mounted blade or barleycorn (an inverted V), often protected by a sheet-steel cover. Luminous and coloured inserts or white beads are also often in vogue. Though opinions change with equal rapidity, anything which can provide contrast against a dark background may be an asset as long as it neither distracts aim nor reflects light.

Optical sights

Open sights had inherent drawbacks; not least were coarse adjustment, poor regulation and the width of the front-sight blade/backsight notch combination, which were often entirely inappropriate for accurate shooting at long range. These problems were exposed as maximum engagement ranges were stretched to 1500 yards, then to 2000 yards or more after the widespread distribution of small-bore cartridges loaded with smokeless propellant.

The initial attempts to satisfy long-range requirements included pendulum, folding bar and elongated ladder sights, typifying a period when complexity was often taken as a mark of technological advance. However, telescope sights had been used successfully during the American Civil War and a Whitworth cap-lock rifle fitted with a Davidson optical sight was tested by the British Army in 1865.

Interest in sights of this type lay dormant for decades, partly owing to cost and partly to their poor optical performance. However, the need for accurate long-range shooting became evident during the Second South African War of 1899–1902, when the Boers,

experienced fieldsmen and often also excellent shots, picked off many British soldiers at great distance. So obvious was this problem that a superstition soon arose that it was unlucky to light three cigarettes from a single match; the Boer, so it was said, saw the first light, aimed at the second and fired at the third.

Though there was a scandal concerning the quality of British rifle sights, sniping attracted official disapproval and nothing was done, except for a few experiments, until the First World War began. The stagnated nature of the Western Front, where the front lines were often well within hailing distance, renewed interest in sniping as a way of picking off enemy officers and reducing morale by confining the men in their trenches. British and Germans alike impressed large numbers of sporting rifles, then progressed to purpose-designed equipment. Not all of the attempts were successful; the so-called Galilean sight proved too fragile – though recently reintroduced by the Israeli Elbit company – and the SMLE lacked long-range accuracy. The Germans made good use of the Mauser, whereas the British, after

pressing old long Lee-Enfields into service, adopted the P14. The Canadian Ross, disappointing though it had proved in combat, also proved exceptionally accurate.

Sniping fell from favour in Britain after the First World War had ended, but interest remained in Germany and, in particular, in the Soviet Union. There the marksman was regarded as an integral part of infantry units and the standard service rifle, the 1891/30-type Mosin-Nagant, performed well enough to be issued in tens of thousands equipped with optical sights made in a factory created in Russia by Zeiss in the late 1920s.

Exploits of snipers during the Second World War contributed to many a successful campaign, from the Russian Front to the Far East, where the Japanese made up what their equipment lacked in quality with their dedication. This highlighted one of the major design criteria, the ability of an optical sight – by definition delicate – to withstand conditions that could range from desert heat or the cold of Siberia to tropical rain forest.

The telescope sight is now customarily made from seamless tube,

A Leupold Vari-X III 3·5-10x50 optical sight, mounted on a Remington Model 700 sporting rifle.

with a diameter of 25mm or 30mm, drawn from aluminium or sheet steel. It can be anodised, blacked, nickelled, chromed, or clad in rubberised armour. The barrel of the sight contains a series of lenses, a reticle and a method of adjusting focus.

Most modern lenses consist of several individual elements even though a cursory glance may suggest them to

be a single unit. The element farthest from the shooter's eye, called the objective, forms the 'primary image' which, but for the inclusion of a separate erector lens, would be inverted. The image passes out through the eyepiece to enter the pupil of the firer's eye.

Optical sights normally magnify the image, but the final size may vary

between a modest 50 per cent gain (1.5x) and a twentyfold increase (20x). Size and weight vary greatly, but a typical 6x40 fixed-magnification sight is 12–13in (305–330mm) long and weighs 11–12oz (310–335g).

Though problems are potentially serious, manufacturing standards are surprisingly high and even the cheapest sights offer acceptable performance –

though the care lavished on the most expensive sights is customarily reflected in their price.

A superior image brightness is obtained in sights with coated lenses, identifiable by their purple-blue or straw colour. Coating is invaluable, as 30 per cent of incidental light may otherwise be lost in the journey through the lenses of an ordinary sight – partly in the glass, but mostly by reflection at the interfaces between air and glass. The best modern sights lose less than 15 per cent of light in this way. Matt-black internal finish minimises reflection losses, though some light still bounces around the sight-tube. In extreme cases, the image may lack colour or display ghosting.

Fields of view can be enlarged by increasing the diameter of the eyepiece lens or shortening the eye relief. Moving the eye nearer the eyepiece is hazardous, however, if powerful cartridges are used and the sights can be driven back into the unwary marksman's face. A 'TV' or wide-screen image may be obtained from rectangular objective lenses; however, unless associated with a suitably enlarged eyepiece or reduced eye relief, the claim may be a sham.

If reticle cross-hairs wander over the target when the head is moved up and down, or from side to side, then the sight is suffering from parallax. Most ordinary telescope sights are corrected for particular distances – usually 100 yards – so that the cross-hairs stay motionless on the target and independent of head movement when aim is taken at this particular range. Adjustable-parallax sights work efficiently if the firer can gauge range

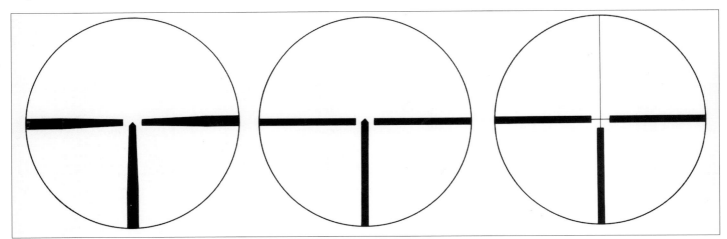

A selection of typical Zeiss Diavari reticles.

This RWS-brand variable-power optical sight, made in Japan, has an illuminated reticle.

accurately, though their value is reduced by setting the corrector for 130 yards when the target proves to be 200 yards away. Parallax cannot occur, however, when the eye, the centre of the reticle and the target image all lie on the longitudinal axis of the sight.

Many reticle designs are available, among the most popular being conventional cross-hairs, cross-hairs and dot, duplex (a combination of thick and thin hairs), cross-on-circle, and vertical post. Illuminated reticles are particularly useful if the levels of brightness can be varied to suit prevailing conditions.

Attempts have even been made to include range-finding features in telescope sights, particularly in military designs though their sporting applications are much less obvious. Illuminated-reticle sights are also useful when shooting into dark ground, especially if the colour of the battery-lit cross-hairs can be altered to suit the prevailing conditions.

Sights are usually supplied with detachable lens caps, the translucent patterns doubling as filters for use on particularly bright days. Others will be encountered with range-finding graticles and some even offer rubberised 'armour', which is very useful for field use.

The British Army currently accepts 4x sights as the best compromise of magnification and field of view, an opinion shared by many fieldsmen. Long-range target shooters, however, may need 24x magnification. Long-tube sights are usually confined to target, bench-rest or vermin shooting. They are rarely durable enough for arduous field use and magnify body tremors so greatly that the image is difficult to stabilise unaided.

Inspired by German experience during the Second World War with the Zf 42 sight, a low-magnification pattern (1.5x) with extraordinarily long eye relief, the Austrian *Bundesheer* has promoted a fixed-focus 1.5x sight since the 1970s. Built into the carrying handle of the Steyr AUG, this is claimed to provide a good field of view, reduce body-tremor effects and allow the firer to keep both eyes open. Most fieldsmen will immediately recognise that the reticle in this sight is much too coarse to place shots accurately at

The British 4x SUSAT optical sight. Note the emergency-use fixed sights on the top of the unit.

long range. Sights with long eye relief remain popular with handgunners, especially those who favour non-magnifying dot reticle patterns for snap-shooting.

Fixed-power sights have given ground to variable-magnification patterns in the 1990s, though 2.5x, 4x, 6x, 8x and 10x are still made in quantity. There has also been a move towards compact scopes. The 3–9x patterns are among the most popular zoom sights, though many alternatives will also be encountered. Variable-power sights are generally heavier and potentially less durable than fixed-power rivals, but such tremendous strides have been made in manufacturing techniques in recent years and this reservation is not as important as it was 20 years ago.

Care should be taken to ensure that focus stays constant throughout the zoom range; there is nothing more annoying than an optical sight (or binocular) that needs constant adjustment as the power changes.

Most of the inherent drawbacks in optical sights arise from flaws in the lenses. Though defective seals can also be troublesome, it is virtually impossible to grind a single-element lens to avoid distortion and problems may still be encountered when multiple elements are used.

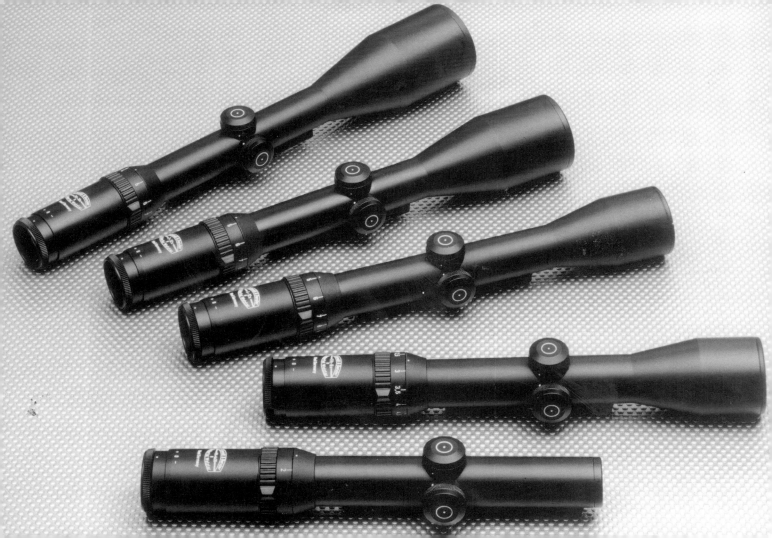

A range of Schmidt & Bender telescope sights. Top to bottom: 2.5–10x56, 3–12x50, 4–12x42, 1.5–6x42 and 1.25–4x20.

Optical sights: problems

Astigmatism is simply an inability to focus lines which cross each other at widely diverging angles. Focusing on chicken wire or similar diagonal-link fences will often reveal if the strands running from left to right are as clear as those running right to left. If no difference can be detected, then there is minimal astigmatism in the lens system. Sights of this type may be labelled 'anastigmatic'.

Chromatic aberration arises from the inability of a lens to focus light rays at a single point. Ordinary white light is composed of a spectrum of colours in which the wavelength, and hence focal length, of each component differs; if the lens is badly corrected, a blurred image with a coloured corona or halo may be visible. Sandwiches of thin glass are used to unify focus, each diffracting or bending a portion of the light at a different angle. If the image is properly focused and no obvious coloured halo or corona effects are visible around small objects, the lens system has been

corrected satisfactorily for chromatic aberration. It will usually be marked 'achromatic'.

Coma occurs when a lens, unable to focus light passing through it obliquely, 'smears' an image outward towards the edges.

Field curvature arises when elements in the lens system, particularly the erector components, produce an image with blurred edges and a pin-sharp centre; or, conversely, a blurred centre with crystal clear margins.

Field of view results solely from dividing the angle of view by the magnification. An enormous objective lens contributes little to performance unless the eyepiece lens is also enlarged. Too restricted a view makes target acquisition difficult; this has little importance in shooting at static targets, but the same cannot be said of combat and it is vital to find a compromise. Variable-magnification or 'zoom' sights are greatly favoured, as they allow a single sight to be used under a variety of conditions, but it must be remembered that the field of view declines as magnification rises. At 100 yards, the field of a sight of this genre drops from 41ft at 3x to only 15ft at 9x; the field of view of an 8–40x56 sight is merely 2.6ft at the highest power.

Image distortion occurs when the lenses have been ground so poorly that parts of the image may seem twisted or bent. Focusing on a brick wall or similar grid-like pattern in the middle distance will show whether horizontal and vertical lines are straight and whether they focus sharply across the entire field of view simultaneously. If the sight passes this examination, the chances are that its lenses have been adequately corrected for coma, field curvature and image distortion. Sights of this type are often termed 'orthoscopic'.

Magnification is simply the relationship between the size of the object seen through the sight compared with that seen with the naked eye. The true magnification can sometimes be gauged by keeping the second eye open and comparing the two images, but this is an unsatisfactory method. Alternatively, a piece of thin paper can be placed over the eyepiece of a sight pointed at a bright light. As the paper is drawn backwards, the circle of light diminishes until it reaches a minimum and then begins to grow. This establishes the eye-point – the optimum distance at which the eye should be placed – and the sight aperture, which is diameter of the circle of light at its smallest point. Magnification can be calculated by dividing the sight aperture into the diameter of the objective lens, though this is prone to give a false figure.

Relative brightness of a particular sight is the square of dividing the effective diameter of the objective lens by the sight aperture. If a 6x telescope sight has an objective lens diameter of 40mm and a sight aperture of 5mm, therefore, then its relative brightness is 64. The limited ability of the human eye ensures that all sights will perform adequately as long as the diameter of the objective lens diameter exceeds 12mm. Large-diameter objectives make no different to resolution of detail, assuming magnification remains unchanged, though they do offer greatly improved transmission of light. Transmission of light is limited by the iris in the human eye, which adjusts automatically to ambient light. But iris diameter rarely exceeds 3mm in daylight and, therefore, any relative brightness greater than 9–10 is wasted: at dusk, conversely, the iris can expand to a little over 5mm for an optimal relative brightness of 25–30. Some large-objective sights may provide relative brightnesses as great as 100, allowing the eye to see detail in conditions where ambient light is

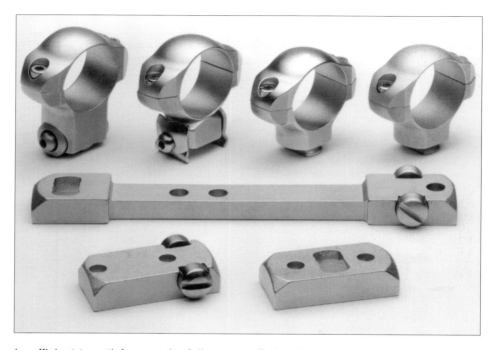

insufficient to satisfy even the fully opened iris.

Resolution of any lens in a small-diameter telescope is limited by the performance of the human eye. A normal eye can resolve detail as fine as a minute of arc, one-sixtieth of a degree (1' or $1/60°$). To find the potential acuity of the eye when presented with a magnified image,

Typical Redfield (American) optical-sight rings and bases.

therefore, the minute of arc is simply divided by the true magnification: a 4x sight would improve the resolution to a quarter of a minute of arc (15 seconds of arc or 15").

Spherical aberration is caused by light rays from the outer margins of the lens focusing ahead of those from the centre, blurring the image. Though this can be minimised by accurate grinding, the work must not disturb essential colour corrections. Lenses have been corrected for spherical aberration if all the differing parts of the image focus simultaneously when adjustments are made. Sights of this type are generally known as 'aplanatic'.

Cutaway drawings of typical Zeiss optical sights.

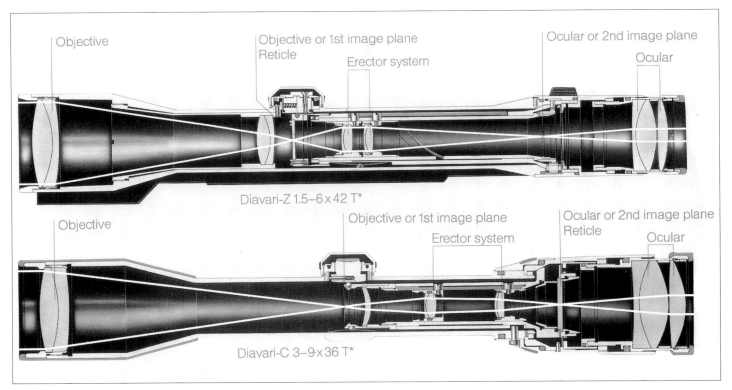

Diavari-Z 1.5–6 x 42 T*

Diavari-C 3–9 x 36 T*

Electro-optical sights

The development of compact image-intensifying systems has been among the most remarkable advances in sighting equipment in recent years and the reduction in price to a point where they cost little more than a good-quality camera has greatly broadened distribution.

The first attempts to improve weapons sights relied on straightforward optical means, magnifying the image so that the target could be seen more clearly. Yet targets could not be engaged in darkness however much the image was enlarged. Some of the best-made telescope sights were capable of improving performance in poor light, it was true, but the gains were limited by the performance of the firer's own eye.

These sights give the impression of being able to see in the dark, but it is important to understand the most basic operating principle. 'Light' is little more than our name for the visible portion of the electromagnetic-radiation spectrum, which ranges from gamma rays at one end (where wavelength is measured in fractions of a nanometre) to ultra-low frequency radio waves measuring several hundred kilometres at the other extreme.

The human eye is capable only of accepting electromagnetic radiation with a wavelength of 390–750nm; though vision varies among individuals, there is comparatively little difference in wavelength response. The eye allows the wavelengths within the limits to be seen in the form of colours, ranging from red (about 700nm), orange (615nm), yellow (585nm), green (530nm), blue (470nm) and violet (about 415nm).

Some animals have much better night vision than we do, which sometimes merely reflects much better light-gathering abilities but in others may be a pushing back of the limits that allow them to see into the near-ultraviolet (short wave) and near-infrared (long wave) spectra. Infrared is particularly useful, as it extends from 700nm to 106nm. However, only the near-infrared portion, 700–900nm, is customarily used in television controls and infrared film. Most video cameras will detect the presence of infrared beams, even though the eye does not. Infrared up to about 2000–2400nm can be used by special cameras. Still longer wavelengths – emitted by 'hot' objects – can be used to create a thermal picture of an item merely by recording the differing emissions of electromagnetic radiation from its surface.

Infrared radiation is simply 'light' that is invisible to our eyes; it can be focused and reflected and can be polarised in the same way as visible light.

One of the first goals was to allow vehicles to move along unlit roads without headlights to betray their presence. The German vehicle-control system known as *Fahrzeug-Gerät* 1229, developed by the Forchungsanstalt der Deutschen Reichspost in collusion with Leitz of Wetzlar, relied on a special converter to present the human eye with an otherwise unseen image by transforming radiation with wavelengths in the near-infrared part of the spectrum.

The night sky was known to contain enough radiation in the near-infrared band to create an image, but the primitiveness of the earliest converters, which were unable to significantly magnify this radiation, resulted in poor resolution. The problems were initially solved by using an infrared lamp to flood the target area, which greatly improved the converted image by providing more reflected light. Now generally known as the 'active' system, this had one great drawback. A suitably equipped opponent could easily detect the presence of the infrared lamp and, by using a passive detector relying simply on reflected light, he could often observe without being seen.

Early in the Second World War, the Germans adapted their driving aid to serve as a rifle sight, the *Zielgerät 1229 Vampir* being mounted on a Kar 98k, a Gew 43, or an MP 43/Stg 44. The equipment consisted of a 13cm-diameter transmitting lamp, the converter and a magnifying eyepiece lens in a telescope-like tube, and a separate electrical supply in the form of a battery pack. *Vampir* units undoubtedly could locate targets in poor light, but only at the expense of excessive dimensions. The power pack alone weighed 15kg (33lb).

By 1945, the US Army had introduced the SniperScope. This worked on the same basic principle as the *Vampir*, but provided the basis for an entirely self-contained passive device; improvements in technology had discarded the infrared floodlight and the battery compartment had been made small enough to be mounted on the sight body. Though the result was heavy, awkward and difficult to handle, it was merely a short step away from the perfection made possible by solid-state electronics.

The greatest single advance made since the Second World War concerns the converter, which was soon developed to a point where it could enhance the image electronically. This gave far better resolution and allowed targets to be engaged confidently at greater distances than the earliest active systems had done.

Most modern intensifier sights follow the same general pattern, though individual details vary greatly.

The SniperScope in action. This picture, taken in May 1957 at Fort Belvoir, Virginia, shows the revised version with the infrared lamp mounted above the sight body.

119

The Soviet-designed NSP-2 infrared weapons sight, mounted on a Czechoslovakian Vz. 58P assault rifle.

Intensifiers of this type may be considered as a television tube inserted in a telescope sight, between the objective and eyepiece lenses. Light from the target – natural or boosted by a floodlight – enters through the objective lens and is focussed on to the front element of the converter. Photons provided by the energy entering from the target image cause electrons to be emitted from the converter's photocathode. These electrons are then focused on to a phosphorescing screen, which in turn emits the photons that give a reconstructed image to the firer's eye.

The key to success was the degree of amplification, releasing as many electrons as possible for each initial photon strike. Though the cascade tubes of the first-generation sights were very bulky, the inclusion of additional intermediate amplification stages gave surprisingly good performance and 60,000-fold gains were not uncommon.

However, the success of image-intensifying sights has been due entirely to the perfection of the photocathode, which is essentially the inside of a window formed as part of a vacuum tube and owes its origins to the photocell and the photomultiplier tubes (PMTs) developed for medical and scientific research. The first PMT was developed by the French Atomic Energy Commission (CEA) in 1953, then improved by the Philips LEP laboratories in Paris (1956). Production began in Brive in the factory now owned by Photonis SA. Many types of PMT have been offered by Photonis and rival companies; and some units have been copied in Russia.

Light radiation from an image is focussed on to the window by conventional lenses, causing electrons to be emitted from the light-sensitive layer. The electrons are then accelerated by a current – usually applied by a small DC battery – to strike a luminescent screen

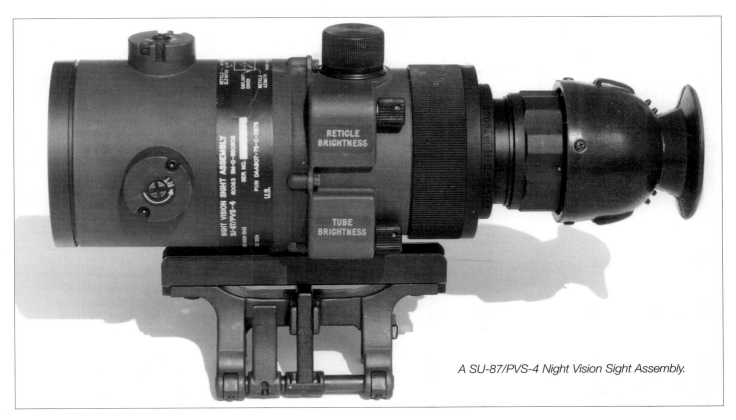

A SU-87/PVS-4 Night Vision Sight Assembly.

forming the inner surface of the rear window of the tube. The phosphor converts electrons back to light radiation and forms an image corresponding to the original but with greatly enhanced brightness. The reconstructed image is normally inverted, but another lens, the ocular, renders it upright before entering the eye.

Though the term 'intensifier' is customarily used for any device of this type, a distinction should rightly be drawn between image converters, which 'convert' an image from the invisible part of the spectrum to an image that can be viewed by the human eye, and image intensifiers, which effectively concentrate an image in the visible spectrum that can be only dimly seen.

Converters and intensifiers have been made in several forms, normally identified as 'generations'. This sometimes gives a clue to their age, but each of the groups possesses merits of its own and first-generation patterns are still being made for specific purposes.

Dating from the mid-1960s, first-generation diodes rely on only a single DC current to accelerate electrons, resulting in excellent image resolution but only a moderate gain in image intensity, usually in the order of 200–500lm/lm (lm = lumen, a measure of brightness per unit area). They can handle images in which the contrast between the light and dark portions is comparatively large and are said to have a 'wide dynamic range' and are comparatively interference-free ('low noise'). The tubes are focussed either by reducing the distance between the photocathode and phosphor screen to a minimum (proximity diode) or by allowing an electron lens to focus the electrons emerging from the photocathode before they reach the luminescent screen. These inverter diodes return the image to its upright form without requiring an additional ocular lens, but are far more clumsy than the proximity type.

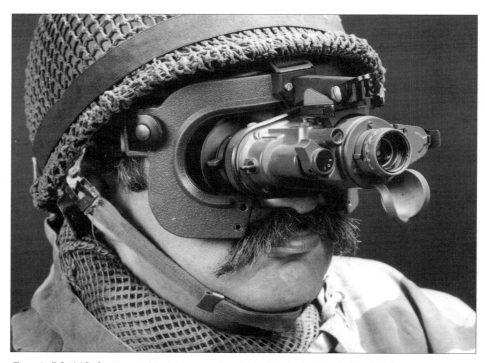

French PC1MC Cyclop night-vision goggles. Note the lack of peripheral vision.

Among the advantages of proximity diodes are the absence of geometric distortion, high resolution over the entire area of the photocathode, and true 1:1 or 'same size' image transfer. They are largely immune to electrical and electromagnetic interference, and can function as ultra-fast opto-electronic shutters in camera equipment.

The Rank Pullin Individual Weapon Sight (IWS) SS20, successfully used by the British Army in Northern Ireland, the Falkland Islands Campaign and elsewhere, typifies first-generation equipment. It is 478mm long, 100mm high, 140mm wide and weighs 2.78kg. Performance included the ability to identify a man-size target at 300m under starlight conditions and to act as a passive infrared detector at 500–600m. However, the great weight of the SS20 (and comparable equipment used elsewhere) added a considerable burden to soldiers armed with the 7.62mm L1A1 rifle; consequently, the SS20/AR-15 or SS20/M16 combination was customarily preferred.

The major drawbacks of these first-generation intensifier sights were expense, excessive size and the delicacy of the converter unit. Improvements in converters, which have now generally changed from cascade-type photocathodes to fibre-optic micro-channel plates, have allowed intensifier sights to be reduced to surprisingly compact dimensions. Their performance remains much the same as their predecessors (perhaps limited by maximum attainable image gain) and the optical components remain largely unchanged, but a considerable reduction in manufacturing costs has been reflected in price.

Second-generation systems may also take proximity- or inverter-diode form. The major change lies in the interposition of a micro-channel plate (MCP), introduced in 1973, between the photocathode and the luminescent screen, enhancing not only the energy of individual electrons but also allowing them to multiply. Electrons from the photocathode pass through tiny holes in a conductive glass plate, rarely more than 10^{-7}mm in diameter. Secondary emissions occur as each electron strikes the sides of the hole; for each electron that enters, ten thousand may emerge. Image resolution and dynamic range suffer by comparison with the first-generation diodes, but luminous gain is far greater: 10,000lm/lm for a single MCP and as much as 10 million (10^7) for two MCPs in stacked configuration.

Typical of second-generation equipment is the Rank Pullin SS86 Crew-served Weapons Sight (CWS), used in conjunction with heavy machine-guns, recoilless guns and some types of vehicle armament. This is capable of 6x magnification, can focus down to 30m and has a view-field of about 6°. The sight measures 365mm overall, has an objective lens diameter of 110mm, and weighs 2.3kg. Power is derived from batteries and the brightness of the illuminated reticle is varied automatically by scene luminescence; the presence of a main battle tank (MBT) can be detected under starlight conditions at 1000m.

Many types of night-viewer are now being made, the Moonlight Mini being among the smallest and most compact designs available. Equipment of this type is particularly useful to armed forces, police and security agencies.

Third-generation diodes are proximity-focus patterns with micro-channel plates and special gallium arsenide photocathodes. These give a better luminous sensitivity (1200 µA/lm instead of 300 µA/lm) than the bi-, tri- and multi-alkali photocathodes used in earlier generations. They are specifically intended for use in infrared and near-infrared spectra and are unsuited to ultraviolet. Their sensitivity makes then susceptible to interference from heat ('thermal noise').

New fourth-generation converters, introduced in the USA by ITT Industries, embody improved manufacturing techniques in a search for more gain and greater resolution. The ITT MX10160B has a 18mm-diameter inversion cathode with a gallium arsenide 'filmless' photocathode bonded to glass; micro-channel plate current amplification; and an inverting fibre-optic phosphor screen. The converter is 1.448in long, with an external diameter of 1.225in, and weighs a few ounces. The MX-10160B can be retrofitted to AN/AVS-6 and AN/AVS-9 helmet sights, to Mini-N/SEAS observation sights, F7001A gunsights and many other intensifiers fitted with second- and third-generation converters.

A basic unit of measurement, the lux, is

defined as the amount of illumination produced when 1 lumen is distributed evenly over an area of 1 square metre; or, alternatively, the illuminance on any point of a surface 1 metre from a point source of 1 candela (1 international candle power). In practical terms, this is generally explained as the level of illumination achieved by good street lighting, or by a full moon on snow or desert sand. By comparison, dusk, with the true colours still largely visible, will increase illuminance by a factor of ten; full sunlight will increase it by 100,000 times or even a million-fold.

Most intensifier sights will black out under even 1-lux conditions unless suitable filters are used, as they are designed to perform under much less favourable conditions. Filtering needs to be excessive if the sights are to remain serviceable in sunlight, otherwise conventional optical equipment must be substituted. Some of the more sophisticated sights can vary the filtering level simply by adjusting the operating voltage, but others require filters to be adjusted manually.

Attempts have been made on night-vision goggles (e.g., Oldelft HNV-1) to provide a satisfactory way of handling low-light and flash-light conditions simultaneously, often with the aid of holographic optical elements (HOEs). This is an area in which rapid advances seem certain to be made.

Intensifiers are at their best in conditions ranging from overcast starlight to full moonlight with light cloud cover. Full moonlight may bring excessive brightness and the beginning of black-out, whereas overcast starlight or unbroken cloud cover may reduce even a third-generation intensifier to impotence in woodland.

Table 1. Performance of British Infantry Weapon Sight (IWS), first-generation inverter-diode type

Light conditions	Illuminance (lux)	Response
Overcast starlight in woodland	10^{-5}	Insufficient light to operate
Overcast starlight in open country	10^{-4}	A weak image is created at maximum objective aperture
Starlight	10^{-3}	Operates well
Moonlight with light cloud cover	10^{-2}	Optimum performance
Full moonlight	10^{-1}	Image uncomfortably bright, unless aperture is reduced
Street lighting or moonlight in snow or desert	1	Sight blacks out at full aperture
Dusk, colours clearly visible	10	Good image with 0.4in-diameter NG3 filter
Overcast or very dull	10^{2}	Optimal image if filtered as described above
Overcast, dull	10^{3}	Sight may black out, even with filter in place
Overcast	10^{4}	Black-out, even with 0.4mm-diameter filter
Sunlight	10^{5}	Black-out
Sunlight on sand or snow	10^{6}	Black-out, unless 0.04in-diameter filter is fitted; not recommended for use except in an emergency

Once restricted to military service and government-funded security organisations, equipment of this type now lies within the grasp of much smaller clients. The Kite Night Sight, made by Pilkington Optronics for service in more than 40 countries, is typical of the 1990s. Equipped with second- or third-generation intensifier tubes, it offers 4x magnification, a view-field of 8° 30' and configurations suited to differing weapons. Two 1.5-volt AA batteries allow continuous use for up to 70 hours.

Kite is 255mm long, has a 73mm-diameter objective lens and weighs about 1200g with its batteries. It has a fixed or adjustable-diopter eyepiece with an eye relief of 30mm and can be focussed from 15m to infinity. The standard second-generation intensifier tube permits a standing-man target to be distinguished under starlight (0.001 lux) conditions out to 300 metres.

Diodes are made only by a handful of companies, including ITT in the USA, NEC in Japan, Photonis in France and Proxitronic (Formerly Bosch-Fernseh) in Germany. Consequently, though there is a surprising variety of branded sighting equipment, the essence of their operation – the converter tube – is simply bought-in when required.

In 2000, for example, Photonis exported to more than 25 countries, sales of this type amounting to more than three-quarters of the company's turnover. Products included the XX1080 first-generation converter, still preferred for vehicle-driver night-vision aids, alongside a variety of second-generation image-intensifier tubes (IITs), including the 50mm diameter XX1300 and the 25mm diameter XX2050. The latter was only 25mm long, or 40mm if the optional fibre-optic expander was requested. XX2050 converters of this type have been used in vehicle telescopes such as the AN/PVS-4, AN/TVS-5 and AN/VVS. They offer simple optics in a small and inexpensive package, which makes them attractive for large-scale use where ultimate sophistication is unnecessary.

Photonis also makes a variety of 18mm-diamater double proximity tubes, commonly substituted in AN/AVS-6, AN/AVS-9, AN/PVS-5, -7A, -7B, -7C and -14 (AN/ANVIS) night-vision goggles. The original second-generation designs, introduced in 1974, have been replaced by the SuperGen® (1985) and HyperGen® (1997) versions.

A British Soldier armed with an L85A1 rifle, demonstrates the complexity and clumsiness of night-vision goggles and laser designator.

Image-intensifier tubes have also proved their value in cameras (still or video), allowing photography in otherwise hostile conditions. The usual method is to provide an alternative lens for existing cameras, though, alternatively, a converter can be placed between an optical lens and the shutter.

Typical of these is the Canon XL-1 with an Optex M3000XL intensifier. Fitted with a Photonis SuperGen® HP inverter diode, it offers a white-light sensitivity of 700 µA/lm, a limiting resolution up to 50 pairs of black/white micro-lines in 1mm, a signal-to-noise ratio (a guide to interference) of 21.5:1 and an average operating life at 500 µlx input of 18,000 hours.

Table 2. Relative detection ranges of PVS-7 system, overcast starlight conditions; vehicle-size target	
Second-generation converters	170m
Third-generation converters	240m (Omni I) to 360m (Omni IV)
Fourth-generation converters	430m

Thermal imagers

Similar to intensifiers in many respects, thermal imagers use infrared radiation to reconstruct an image based on differences in the heat signature of the components of an object. The night sky contains considerably more electromagnetic radiation in the near-infrared spectrum than in the limited window in which the human eye performs best. However, the phosphor present in the target emits photons at wavelengths similar to the sensitivity of a dark-adapted or 'scotopic' eye.

The first sights to be perfected had one important drawback. The poor performance of the photocathode in the converter systems required the areas under observation to be flooded with infrared light before the image could be relayed satisfactorily to an observer's eye. This was acceptable as long as sights remained in short supply, or were restricted to just one side. However, without the light switched on, infrared sights can act as passive detectors. Once sights of this type are widely distributed, they effectively lose their value.

One result has been the substitution of thermal-imaging systems. A problem to be overcome during development was that, even over the distances relevant to surveillance or military engagement, thermal emissions from potential targets is customarily absorbed or scattered by the atmosphere before it can reach the observer. Fortunately, two narrow wavebands were discovered (approximately 3000–5000nm and 8000–13,000nm) where thermal emissions penetrate the atmosphere efficiently and the sights can perform much better than those relying on infrared spectra.

Unfortunately, thermal-imaging sensors need to be cooled continuously (often relying on liquid nitrogen) and are usually bulky. The reconstructed image looks odd, lacking definition and often bizarrely coloured, but is often suitable for observation of, for example, whether a tank is static or on the move. Attempts have been made to combine thermal imagers with image-intensifiers, seeking to combine the strengths of each system to cloak the other's weakness.

Officine Galileo offered a thermal imaging/image intensifying sight in the 1980s, which had the ability to superimpose the infrared and thermal-emission images to improve performance. Though production has now ceased, there may yet be development potential in multi-system sights of this type.

Typical of its class, the Lasergage Hand Held Thermal Imaging System (HHTI) can resolve temperature differentials as small as 1°C. Designed to operate in the 3–5 micron spectral band, it has .75x magnification, a 21° viewfield, and measured approximately 27x17x17cm. A night-sight variant, the Lasergage LWS 1060, claimed to be able to engage man-size targets in low-light conditions at 300m. Minimal focus was 25m, magnification was 3.5x, and the field of view was about 8°. The sight could be adapted to fit a variety of small arms. It was 265mm long, had a 75mm-diameter objective lens and weighed 895g.

Laser rangers

The basis of many modern targeting systems is a laser beam, though the details vary greatly from manufacturer to manufacturer. The principle of the laser has been known for many years, but the first commercially practicable system (based on rods of ruby) was not perfected until the early 1960s.

The name 'laser' is an acronym of 'light amplified by stimulated emission of radiation'. The basic principles involve exciting individual atoms with a beam of light to generate additional radiation in phase with the light beam, which is thus reinforced. The results can be magnified to produce a beam of coherent (i.e. single frequency) light of great power.

This system has been widely touted as the 'death ray' beloved by science fiction, though this technology has yet to be perfected. A more accessible benefit has been the development of continuous one-line projectors used for alignment and surveying tasks. Lasers of this type, usually gas-discharge patterns, inspired the development of aiming projectors. The visible lasers customarily rely on an excited helium-neon mixture, whereas infrared designs may use carbon monoxide or even hydrogen cyanide.

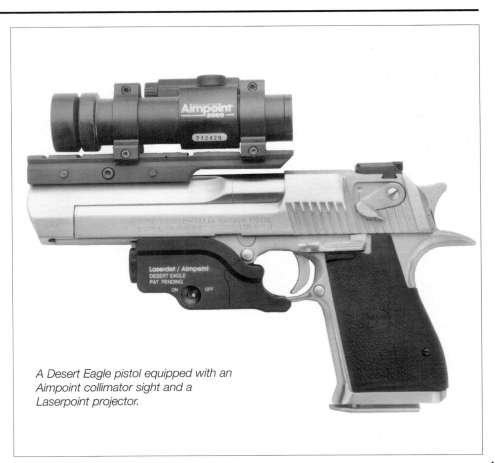

A Desert Eagle pistol equipped with an Aimpoint collimator sight and a Laserpoint projector.

Some laser designators operating in the visible spectrum project a beam which can be seen by the firer and the target at all times, whilst others operate in the infrared bands and require an additional detector in the form of a headset. Headsets are usually equipped with monocular intensifier-type detector tubes, often disguised with binocular eyepieces. These allow the firer to look away from the target whenever necessary, instead of demanding continuous observation of the target. When a target is selected, relying on the headset to create the illusion of daylight under starlit conditions, the designator is activated and an aiming mark appears on the target. Assuming the sights are properly adjusted for range, the shot will strike the aiming mark without requiring undue concentration on the part of the firer.

A typical laser-assisted designator, made by Pilkington in the early 1990s, operated on a wavelength of 820nm. Powered by two small batteries and weighing merely 340g, it projected a red dot out to 500m, which, in conjunction with an image intensifier, greatly accelerated target acquisition.

Designator systems undoubtedly improve shooting skills, particularly snap-shooting, but the designator unit

This Ruger KP94 has a laser designator built into the front of the frame.

must be activated to obtain a sighting mark and proceeding too leisurely can encourage counter-sniping. Restrictions are also placed on peripheral vision by headset construction.

Collimator and other sights

Though image-intensifying sights have made tremendous progress in recent years, they are still expensive compared with optical sights. Beginning with the late lamented Singlepoint, introduced in the 1970s, attempts have been made to enhance snap-shooting with sighting equipment which relies on an optical illusion.

Collimator sights combine an aiming mark within the sight body, illuminated either by ambient light or by electrical batteries, with the ability of the firer's binocular eyesight to accommodate the reflected aiming mark and a view of the target simultaneously.

Singlepoint appeared to be projecting a red dot on to the target and undoubtedly facilitated rapid fire, but few of these sights – even those with powered reticles – have proved to be of much use in darkness. Ambient-light reflectors are also generally ineffective under dark-to-light conditions.

The collimator sights lost favour for much of the early 1990s, even though the South African Armson OES (Occluded Eye Sight) had been touted with surprising vigour. However, FN Herstal is currently promoting a powered

A Swedish-made Aimpoint collimator sight. This particular example is intended for a bow, which can sometimes be used by special forces.

sight of this general class on its P90® Individual Weapon and the Trijicon ACOG reflex sight, originally tested by the US Army for compatibility with the

Close Combat Soldier Enhancement Program, has found a special forces niche. The intensity of the amber-colour aiming dot of the ACOG reflex unit

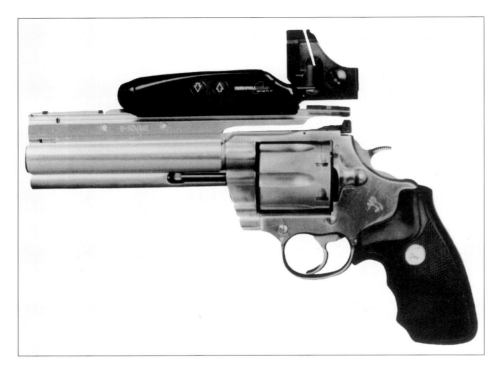

A Bushnell HOLOsight mounted on a Colt Python revolver.

Light projectors in the form of small torches can be mounted on firearms. Often attached beneath the fore-end of a rifle, they are too large for small pistols unless the bottom of the magazine can be adapted as shown with this Glock.

adjusts automatically to light conditions, being powered by a combination of ambient light and a tritium lamp.

Another advance is the Bushnell HOLOsight, which makes use of a laser-generated hologram to project virtually any two- or three-dimensional reticle. The HOLOsight uses a microprocessor to control shut-down mode and the selectable brightness /start-up settings. One of the most interesting features is the three-dimensional 'rising dot', which gives the illusion of projecting a line from the gun barrel to end in a dot beneath a half-circle reticle.

Light projectors will also be encountered on firearms, ranging from purpose-built illuminators to small Mag-Lite™ type torches.

EDGED WEAPONS

Many commentators have written off the value of bayonets in recent years on the grounds that the form of combat that gave rise to them in the seventeenth century – and had sustained them in front-line service to the Korean War and beyond – no longer applies to a war fought by computers.

Bayonets were introduced to compensate for the inefficiency of cap- and flint-lock firearms, giving a close-quarters defence if the firer was unable to reload or had run out of ammunition. The tapered hafts of knives were simply rammed into gun muzzles, but were soon replaced by 'ring' and 'socket' designs that sensibly allowed guns to be fired with their bayonets in place.

The tubular socket bayonet, with the blade set out of the line of fire, was exceptionally popular. It lasted in general service into the second half of the nineteenth century and survives today for use on the FAL. However, with a few minor exceptions, socket bayonets were suitable only for thrusting. They were also comparatively weak and could be bent or broken by a determined twist. Consequently, excepting the Russians and the Soviets (whose infantrymen remained wedded

to socket bayonets until 1945), most armies had moved to sword, sabre and knife bayonets by 1900.

A legacy of the socket bayonet may be seen in the folding bayonets fitted to many Soviet M1944/Chinese Type 53 Mosin-Nagant carbines, Chinese Type 56 Simonov (SKS) carbines, Chinese-made Type 56-1 Kalashnikov assault rifles still in use in Afghanistan and elsewhere across the world and the Chinese Types 63, 68, 73 and 81 militia rifles. Similar bayonets, with knife-type blades, distinguished the SKS made in the Soviet Union, the German Democratic Republic and what was once Yugoslavia.

The introduction of short rifles such as the SMLE was accompanied by a reversion to long-bladed sword bayonets, usually so that men would not be at a reach disadvantage against a conventionally armed enemy, but this concept was being challenged when the Second World War began. One solution was the cheap mass-produced spike bayonet issued in Britain, though this was little more than an updated socket bayonet; another was to develop a general-purpose knife that could be fitted to a rifle when required.

Among the most obvious examples of the latter course was the US M4 bayonet, developed in retrospect to fit the .30 M1 Carbine. The gun had been developed specifically to arm non-combatants, but rapidly found a place in the front line as a substitute for the pistol. As demands for bayonets were soon being heard from combat units and as production ultimately exceeded 6 million, the US Army authorities relented.

The cross-guard of the M3 general-purpose/fighting knife was extended to incorporate a muzzle ring and a double pivoting-arm locking mechanism was enclosed in the pommel. Approved in May 1944, the M4 bayonet-knife was ordered into immediate full-scale production and work on the M3 ceased.

Another example of a last-minute reintroduction occurred when the *Wehrmacht* demanded the addition of an under-muzzle lug on the prototype MKb 42 (H) assault rifle to receive the standard Kar 98k-type knife bayonet.

The US Army M4 was extremely successful, though the leather-washer grips tended to rot in Far Eastern theatres, where heat and humidity promoted fungal infestation. However,

after first moulded rubber and eventually two-piece injection-moulded plastic grips had been perfected, the problem was overcome. M4-type bayonets are still being made in a slightly modified form (as the M7) for the AR15/M16 ArmaLite series and an M3-type knife has reappeared. In addition, the standardisation by NATO of the US-type grenade launcher, and also often the accompanying bayonet lug, has led to the introduction of indigenous variants of the M7 destined for rifles such as the Argentine FARA 83, the Singaporean SR-88A and even (customarily as an option) with the Austrian-made Steyr AUG.

Another innovation with pre-1945 origins is the bayonet-tool. Though origins can be seen in the combination bayonets/wire-cutters invented during the First World War – few of which ever made the transition from drawing-board to service in the trenches – the prototype was the German SG 42, introduced in 1944. Made in Solingen by Carl Eickhorn Waffenfabrik, this had a detachable tool insert in its pressed-steel grip supplied by Robert Klass (code 'ltk'). The insert contained a short knife blade with a bottle opener and a small eye, a second blade with a screwdriver tip and a wire-stripping notch, a corkscrew and a bradawl.

Another landmark was the development of a reinforced scabbard that, in conjunction with a hole in the bayonet-blade, could double as a wire-cutter. It was a short step to include insulation, allowing the owner to cut electrified fences. The first to produce a design of this type in quantity seems to have been the Soviet Union, with the bayonet-tool for the AKM; this seems to have appeared in the late 1960s, but was soon copied in the West.

At the end of the twentieth century, attitudes to the bayonet remained in a state of flux. Realising that bayonets have an adverse effect on accuracy, some armies have discarded this type of weapon in favour of purpose-designed general-purpose or combat knives. Others are convinced of the merits of combining as many functions as possible in one unit. The Russians have ever offered a multi-purpose knife/tool with a single-shot pistol built into the grip! However, the bayonet has important psychological advantages. The Eickhorn catalogue of 1996, for example, stated that 'During counterinsurgency operations, there are almost always times when suspicious haystacks, thatched roofs, piles of rubbish or other potential hiding places have to be checked. Using a bayonet on the end of the rifle,

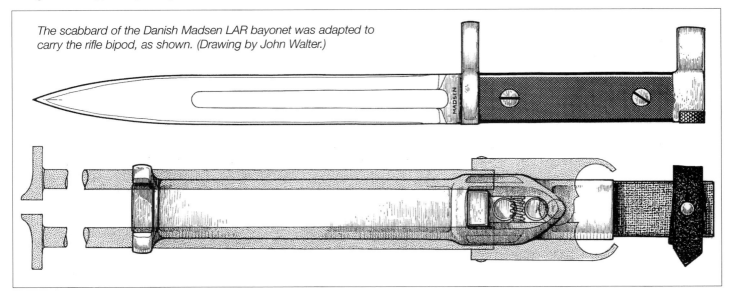

The scabbard of the Danish Madsen LAR bayonet was adapted to carry the rifle bipod, as shown. (Drawing by John Walter.)

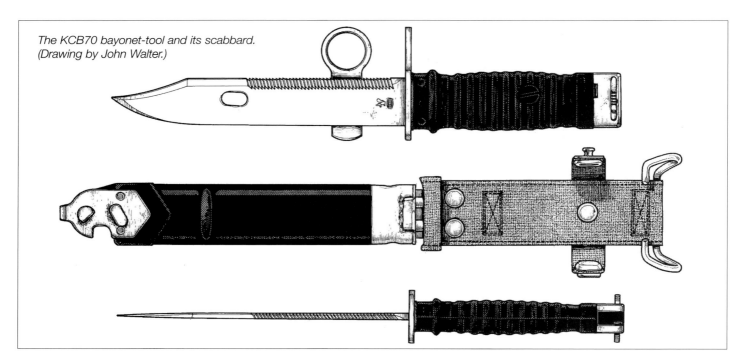

The KCB70 bayonet-tool and its scabbard. (Drawing by John Walter.)

for instance…gives the option of firing immediately should a target be exposed, while the sharp edge at…[the]…muzzle prevents the target pulling the weapon out of [the searcher's] hands'.

The bayonet-tool is inevitably a compromise, as the space required to accommodate tools usually makes the grip far too bulky and angular to offer a good grip. The combat knives are inevitably far better for knife fighting and attempts have been made to fit the tools into sheaths and scabbards (where they run the risk of loss) so that the knife grip can be optimised.

The Israeli army was once pilloried for including a bottle-opener on the Galil rifle bipod – an eminently sensible idea in desert conditions! – and the British still issue a tube-handled wire-cutter/knife bayonet with the L85A1. The French FAMAS accepts a ungainly knife bayonet with a supplementary muzzle ring on the pommel; the Germans issued a distinctive bayonet with the G3,

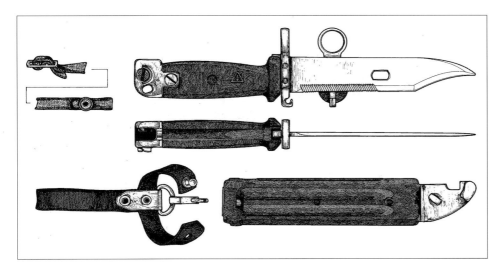

The AKM bayonet-tool and its scabbard. (Drawing by John Walter.)

though the new G36 accepts a variant of the US M7; the Swiss use a bayonet-tool with the Stg 90; the Russians use a wire-cutter bayonet with the AK-74M and the hundred-series Kalashnikovs. Much of the novelty concerns the methods of fixing the bayonet to the rifle; though the muzzle ring is now all but universal, some bayonet pommels rely on conventional T-bar and slot attachments whereas others rely on pivoting latches and projecting circular bosses.

The Swedish Army has abandoned the bayonet in favour of the knife, a trend the increasing interest in short 'personal weapons' such as the FN P90® may soon accelerate. Yet the idea of a bayonet-tool remains attractive, particularly if the knife can retain a good shape and the tools are sturdy enough. Compromise is inevitable, however, and some of those that are currently being made are too flimsy, too complicated or too clumsy to be satisfactory. This is partly due to the need to pass acceptance tests that would defeat many of even the finest combat knives.

A typical bayonet-tool case history is presented by the KCB-70, developed by Eickhorn in the 1960s to accompany the Stoner weapons family and still being made in a variety of guises. Most armies now buy in bayonets from specialist suppliers, resulting in a commonality of parts; only muzzle and pommel fittings need to be changed, whereas each type of rifle once had a distinctive bayonet of its own. Consequently, the KCB-70 is being offered in a variety of subvariants.

Combat, pocket and tool knives are also popular, personal preference often being the ultimate arbiter. Combat knives are often bought from well-known manufacturers such as K-Bar, while the Leatherman- and Gerber-multi-bladed combination tools are also popular.

GRENADES

The idea of projecting grenades (small explosive projectiles) from firearms is by no means new, dating back at least to the eighteenth century and the raising of grenadier regiments in many armies. These ancient grenades were usually fired from cups attached to the muzzles of short carbine-like musketoons, relying on the flash of the propellant to ignite a fuze in the base of a projectile that customarily took the form of a sphere. The performance of these bombs was erratic, owing to the unpredictable burning qualities of individual fuzes and partly because the flash of the propellant in the gun bore sometimes failed even to ignite the fuze.

A combination of erratic ignition, short range and poor explosive capacity soon brought the flirtation with firearms as grenade launchers to an end. Consequently, until the twentieth century, grenades were either thrown or projected as mortar shells.

This situation changed with the introduction of the first modern designs, shortly after the end of the Russo-Japanese War in 1905. The British Army adopted the Hales rifle grenade (Grenade No. 3) in early 1915, while the Germans had accepted a rod-type

grenade of their own in 1913. These designs relied on blank cartridges to fire grenades with stick-like tails that extended back down into the rifle bore. However, consistently firing rifles in this way placed great strain on their construction and, ultimately, specially

reinforced weapons were issued. In addition, the firer had to remember to change ammunition; firing a ball round instead of a special grenade-launching blank courted disaster, as the momentary rise in pressure that occurred as the bullet was stopped by the tail-rod of the

Typical Dynamit Nobel (DAG) 40mm grenades.

An Australian F88 (Steyr AUG) assault rifle, firing an ADI rifle grenade.

grenade was quite sufficient to blow the rifle apart.

An alternative, therefore, was to issue special grenades that could be launched with a ball cartridge, deliberately allowing the small fast-moving bullet to pass out through an axial port in the grenade body. This method worked well enough, but had a major disadvantage: though the major projectile flew a few hundred yards, the bullet could continue for another 2 miles, retaining sufficient energy to remain an unwanted threat.

Some inventors proposed yet another way, hoping to trap a bullet within the shaft of the grenade and thus achieve the ideal solution: use of standard ammunition, but without the unwanted long-range danger of a 'through bullet' design. This left only the necessity for special grenade-launching sights and an assortment of auxiliary and clip-on designs have been tried over the past 80 years. The problem remains with modern rifles, though attempts have been made to fit disposable sights on the grenades themselves.

Modern rifle-projected grenades may work with any of the three major launching systems: blank, through-bullet or bullet trap. None of these solutions is ideal, though all work effectively enough. The Mecar 35x40 HE-RFL BTU may be taken as typical. It is 288mm overall, weighs 387g and contains a 54g explosive charge. The jacket fragments into 300 parts, with a lethal radius of 5m and a maximum wounding radius of 20m. A velocity of about 63m/sec when projected from a 5.56mm FN FNC gives an operational range of 200m, though the maximum distance, depending on the type and calibre of gun, may exceed 300m

The supply of rifle grenades gives quartermasters yet another problem, especially if they also need special blank ammunition. An alternative method is to provide a special launcher in the form of a large-diameter gun, which should be

The Russian AGS-17 Plamya *automated grenade launcher.*

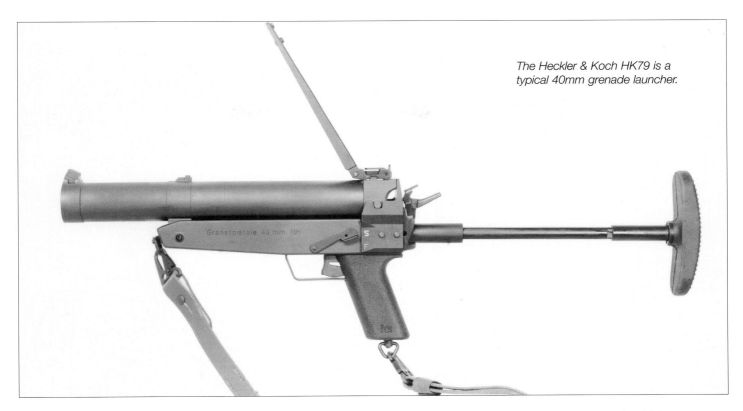

The Heckler & Koch HK79 is a typical 40mm grenade launcher.

light enough to be carried on an infantry rifle. The US Army issued large numbers of the purpose-designed single shot M79 launcher in Vietnam, which took the form of a short single-barrel break-open shotgun firing a 40mm-diameter shell.

This was possible largely because of improvements in ammunition – in particular, the adaptation of the high/low pressure principle, exploited in Germany during the Second World War for artillery, to small arms. A small amount of

propellant was burned at high pressure in a confined space within a cartridge case, then allowed to bleed into a larger space (which was then occupied at low pressure) and drive the grenade out of the muzzle.

A 5.56mm HK41 fitted with a grenade launcher, which substitutes for the fore-end.

This basic principle was adapted by Colt to provide the CGL-4 launcher, tested in action on AR-15/M16 rifles and found wanting. This was replaced by the M203, which proved to be much more efficient and is still in service. Consequently, many other gunmakers have adopted the 40mm grenade round, some favouring purpose-built gun-like launchers and others fitting add-on launchers to rifles. The Soviet Union has followed the US lead by adapting the 30mm round fired by the AGS-17 Plamya

automated launcher to suit the Kalashnikov and there have been many other designs.

The Heckler & Koch 40mm high-explosive fragmentation grenade is typical of this class. The round is 99mm long, weighs 230g and a 180g projectile is fired at 76m/sec (5.56mm H&K G41). The grenade contains 700 2.25mm-diameter steel balls and an explosive charge of about 30g Hexal 70/30. Lethal radius is 5m; maximum effective wounding radius is 15m and the

maximum engagement range is about 350m. A self-destruction device is activated ten seconds after the grenade has been fired.

Additional information about hand-thrown grenades, including explosive and gas patterns, can be found in other Greenhill Military Manuals – Will Fowler, *The World's Elite Forces: Arms and Equipment* (2001) and Ian Hogg, *Ammunition: Small arms, Grenades and Projected Munitions* (1998).

SILENCERS

The idea of a silent firearm has interested many people, particularly as an assassination tool; the airgun, for example, was being regarded with suspicion as early as the seventeenth century (being banned by many authorities) and Napoleon Bonaparte is said to have ordered any sharpshooter captured with a Girandoni-system butt-reservoir gun to be executed without trial.

The idea of silent firearms lay dormant as long as black powder was used, but the advent of smokeless propellant had the paradoxical effect of both increasing noise (thanks to the supersonic crack) and simultaneously increasing interest in reducing the noise, which was possible only because of the design of the new self-contained ammunition.

Inspiration may have been provided by the necessity to muzzle the barking exhaust of the earliest internal-combustion engines. However, the gun-silencer is a comparatively recent invention, the first effectual patent being issued to Maxim in 1908. The British tested the Maxim design in 1910 and the US Army had issued small numbers prior to the First World War. Others were tested experimentally, but, by 1918, none had been efficient enough to attract large-scale purchases.

The problems concerned length, weight and the speed with which the baffle plates wore out. Not until the period between the wars was much progress made, but most revolved around the use of low-power subsonic ammunition that was anathema to most military minds. The Soviet authorities issued low-power 'Partisan' ammunition during the Second World War, for use with Mosin-Nagant rifles, but these relied more for their success on the difficulty of locating the firer than the performance of any silencer (though some guns were undoubtedly so fitted).

The Germans developed a special assassination carbine, with a full-length silencer shrouding the barrel, and attempts were made elsewhere. The US Army purchased silenced High-Standard pistols for the OSS and the British developed the Welrod for the SOE. It was on the success of these pioneering efforts that many post-war designs have been based.

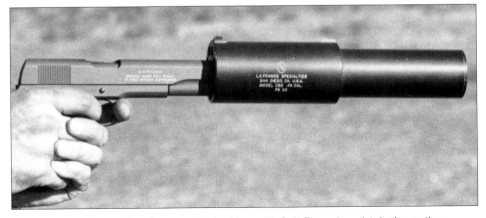

This LaFrance Specialties silencer, attached to a .45 Colt-Browning pistol, shows the traditional drawbacks of equipment of this type: size and weight.

Revolvers are difficult to silence, owing to the gap between the chamber and the barrel, but attempts have been made. This specially modified 5.56mm Ruger GP has a Knight's Armament Company silencing unit.

The ready availability of silencers through commercial channels has ensured a steady supply to police and criminals alike, but it must be said that no silencer can reduce the report of a full-power cartridge to nothing. Tests have often shown a considerable fall in noise levels, but this is instead of reduction elimination. The goal is more to prevent an observer locating the firer, often done only at the cost of surprising complexity. Though some silencers have relied simply on rubber washers to retain gas after the bullet has passed, leaking the contents gently to the atmosphere once their pressure and heat had dissipated, these systems last only a few shots before the hole pierced in the washer enlarges to a point where the spill-over of propellant gas follows the bullet out of the muzzle.

An alternative to the traditional silencer-equipped firearm is provided by the development of the 'piston cartridge', patented in the early 1900s, tested by the US Army in the 1960s under the name Whisper, and now chambered in some Soviet/Russian weapons. This achieves its goal by confining the gas within the cartridge case.

When these guns fire, the rapid increase of pressure within the case not only starts the bullet off on its journey along the bore but also then pushes a

The British have used a silenced Sterling submachine-gun, the L34A1, which replaced the Mk 6 silenced Sten. The US Armed Forces have issued the Smith & Wesson Hush Puppy and the new Heckler & Koch SOCOM pistol; the Soviet Union made use of a silenced Makarov and Stechkin pistols before moving on to a remarkable variety of purpose-built silent weapons; Heckler & Koch have built a variety of silenced MP5 submachine guns.

Even full-length rifles have been fitted with suppressors, often giving the appearance of a large-diameter barrel casing. Unlike a true silencer, which tries to reduce the velocity of the bullet and the propellant gases to subsonic levels, suppressors are designed solely to reduce gas velocity. Bullets still emerge from them at supersonic speed, and the 'crack' is still evident, but there is no secondary trace in the form of gas emerging from the muzzle supersonically or muzzle flash.

An Accuracy International PM sniping rifle with a full-length suppressor unit.

The Heckler & Koch SOCOM pistol fitted with its in-line silencer and laser designator.

plug into the case mouth, acting as a surprisingly good temporary seal that has leaked sufficiently by the time the breech opens to have dropped to a safe level.

Piston-cartridge guns are more or less silent and, lacking the traditional large-diameter body, can be exceptionally compact. The Russian 7.62x42 'Pistol,

Silent Complex', for example, weighs 700g with an empty six-round magazine and is merely 165mm long.

ABBREVIATIONS

ACOG *Advanced Combat Optical Gunsight*
ACR *Advanced Combat Rifle*
AK *Automat Kalashnikova*
AMR *Anti-Materiél Rifle*
AVF *Avtomaticheskaya Vintovka Fedorova*
AVS *Simonov Automatic Rifle*
CAL *Carabine Automatique Légere*
CAW *Close Assault Weapon*
CEA *French Atomic Energy Commission*
CETME *Centro de Estudios Técnicos de Materiales Especiales*
CWS *Crew-served Weapons Sight*
DAO *Double-action Only*
GEOS *Grupos Especiales de Operaciónes*
GIS *Gruppo Intervenzione Speciale*
GPMG *General-Purpose Machine-Gun*
HHTI *Hand Held Thermal Imaging System*

HOE *Holographic Optical Element*
IIT *Image-Intensifier Tube*
IW *Individual Weapon*
IWS *Individual Weapon Sight*
JSSAP *Joint Service Small Arms Program*
LRS *Laser Rifle Scope*
LSW *Light Support Weapon*
MBT *Main Battle Tank*
MCP *Micro-Channel Plate*
MILSPEC *Military Specification*
NATO *North Atlantic Treaty Organisation*
NOCS *Nucleo Operativo Centrale di Sicurezza*
OCIW *Objective Combat Infantry Weapon*
OES *Occluded Eye Sight*
OHWS *Offensive Handgun Weapons System*

PDW *Personal-Defence Weapon*
PMT *Photomultiplier Tube*
RMR *Revolver Manurhin-Ruger*
RPD *Ruchnoi Pulemet Degtyareva*
RPK *Ruchnoi Pulemet Kalashnikova*
SFMG *Sustained-Fire Machine-Gun*
SKS *Samozariadniya Karabina Simonova*
SMLE *Short, Magazine, Lee-Enfield Rifle*
SOCOM *Special Operations Command*
SPAS *Special Purpose Automatic Shotgun*
SPIW *Special Purpose Individual Weapon*
STANAG *Nato Standardised fitting*
SWAT *Special Weapons And Tactics*
TMP *Tactical Machine Pistol (Steyr)*
UMP *Universal-Maschinen-Pistole*
WLAR *Winchester Light Automatic Rifle*